Managing
the Matrix

Managing the Matrix

The secret to surviving and thriving
in your organization

A MENTOR'S TALE

Dawn Metcalfe

WILEY

This edition first published 2014
© 2014 Dawn Metcalfe

Registered office
John Wiley and Sons Ltd, The Atrium, Southern Gate, Chichester, West Sussex, PO19
8SQ, United Kingdom

For details of our global editorial offices, for customer services and for information
about how to apply for permission to reuse the copyright material in this book please see
our website at www.wiley.com.

Library of Congress Cataloging-in-Publication Data

Metcalfe, Dawn,
    Managing the matrix: the secret to surviving and thriving in your organization / Dawn
Metcalfe.
        pages cm
    ISBN 978-1-118-76537-1 (cloth)
1. Matrix organization.   2. Employees—Mentoring of.   3. Performance.   4. Personnel
management.   I. Title.
    HD58.5.M47 2014
    650.1—dc23   2013047058

A catalogue record for this book is available from the British Library.

ISBN 978–1–118–76537–1 (hardback) ISBN 978–1–118–76534–0 (ebk)
ISBN 978–1–118–76535–7 (ebk)

Cover design: Simon Goggin

Set in 11.5/15 pt ACaslonPro-Regular by Toppan Best-set Premedia Limited, Hong Kong
Printed in Great Britain by TJ International Ltd, Padstow, Cornwall, UK

To my new friend Boris. You kept me going when things got hard. Thank you.

CONTENTS

Introduction

Working in the matrix is hard. That's what anybody I've ever spoken to who works in one says. Many of them say that it is the only option, however. They recognize opportunities exist in the matrix; but almost every person and a significant amount of research point to turf wars, confusion over accountability, competing geographical and functional targets, lack of clearly defined roles, and too many people involved in the decision-making process, as some of the problems caused or exacerbated by working in a matrix.

To find out how best to deal with these issues I have talked to hundreds of managers, directors and executives during training courses and coaching sessions. I've formally interviewed dozens of individuals entrenched in organizations that use the matrix structure. The answer seems to be that the "soft" skills we often wait to train people on until after they need them are key to success in the matrix and, possibly, in any job.

This book is a story about Johann, a senior manager, recently converted believer in "soft" skills and desperate to keep

Debra, a high-potential, highly educated member of "Gen Y" who feels like she's not getting enough attention. It asks whether emotional intelligence (EI) exists and, if it does, how is it useful in working within a matrix? And of course, if it exists and is useful, then can we learn it?

My story is based on what I have learned from clients, many of whom work in a matrix organization. What is striking is the similarity of their experiences across industry, job function, level in the organization, cultural background, age or sex. It appears that it's always difficult to get people from different cultural backgrounds (whether nationality or functional or organizational) to do what you want when you don't understand why they resist, especially if you can't force them and have no control over their pay or conditions.

The personalities and events in this book are not based on any individual but reflect the stories I have heard and the situations I have seen over the years. The issues are challenging because to resolve them you need what the best leaders and companies have, and what the Corporate Leadership Council identified as playing a critical role in the matrix – strong communication skills, teamwork, adaptability, and shared goal and rewards systems. Without these (and they are not easy to get) the issues most commonly faced are lack of accountability, frequent conflicts over allocation of resources, and division of authority – none of which are good for the bottom line.

Johann and Debra exhibit a mixture of all the great attributes I see in my clients – listening, questioning, open-mindedness, generosity, thoughtfulness, determination, and pragmatism. Of course they aren't perfect but then who is? Their faults and opinions are all entirely made up of course.

The matrix isn't going away: in a European survey conducted by Krauthammer, an international professional services company, published in 2006, 85 per cent of people said that some form of matrix was present in their organization. This leaves us with two choices – to devote as much time and energy to honing the "soft" skills that lead to personal and organizational success as we do to building our technical skills or to rail against the tides like King Canute. I hope this book persuades you to do as Johann does.

I

The Challenge is Set

Johann Spilk was frazzled. He couldn't understand why he'd done it. Why had he just staked his reputation on something that he had only just been convinced himself would work? He sighed.

Shrugging off his jacket, he hung it up before greeting a couple of colleagues. Then he checked in with his assistant (as always, here before him and already organized for the day ahead), sat down behind his desk and took a sip of the over-priced and highly calorific coffee he'd started drinking since giving up smoking during Ramadan a few months ago. He turned on the computer screen and logged in, ready to prepare for his day of meetings.

Johann's first meeting was with Debra, a young "up and comer" currently doing a rotation in the finance department working on a company-wide project. He didn't really know much about her as they had never come into contact.

At a workshop the previous week, Debra had been identified both as "talent" and "at high risk". In other words, she was doing her current job really well and was likely to be able to move up at least two levels in the next three years, but was known to be actively looking for a new job. The exec team wanted to keep her but she had just been turned down for a promotion as they felt she wasn't ready for the next role yet.

So far so good. But then Johann had had the bright idea of suggesting that she be given a place on a new mentoring programme he had set up.

Background: about two years ago the new HR director at the time, Amy, had flagged up a trend where the time taken to get new hires up to speed was taking longer with each intake. And, then, when they *did* get them functionally competent, the best of those people were disappearing. When HR asked them why they were leaving, the most common response was that they weren't getting the development they wanted and were going somewhere smaller. They felt like they were slipping between the cracks and not learning.

The company decided to create a training programme where money was spent on an online university. Employees could now watch multimedia presentations and earn credits for undergoing training courses. Some of these courses were made mandatory to emphasize the importance. This initiative worked well for technical training, but the behaviours that the programme was meant to address – giving feedback and helping employees develop – hadn't changed. In fact, it was found that, after training, most people reverted to their standard way of behaving within a few weeks, especially if their own managers didn't support them.

Johann had been travelling on the day that a task force had been set up to deal with this and so, obviously, he had been "volunteered". The "task force chief" (he cringed) had asked him to investigate and come up with some solutions. One of the things on the list of recommendations had been mentoring. Johann did a bit more research, engaged in training and, despite himself, had become convinced of its merits.

After 20 years of managing others in different multinational companies, in different locations, preceded by 10 years in the army where he believed he received the best training money could buy, Johann had approached the mentoring course with what he would describe as "some scepticism". Others might regard it as hostility. Despite himself, however, he found it was helpful to have a basic model or theory to refer to when working with others, and it offered a chance to practise important behaviours.

The idea he was mainly interested in – and so the area he tended to work with most with his mentees – was emotional intelligence (EI). He didn't claim to be an expert but rather an interested layperson who believed, after doing his homework, that EI was somehow key to the success of individuals in a matrix organization. He came to realize that EI might be the only tool beyond being skilled at your job that works. He was starting to believe that you could teach EI by using it, and by being transparent about using it, during mentoring or coaching.

Setting up the programme had proved quite a battle. The CFO, Sara, had already described it as a "colossal waste of money" and on mention of his new mentee Debra, she had simply huffed, "that's a great idea" in a sarcastic tone. Johann had decided that he'd had enough of her snide comments and said so.

From there things had disintegrated into an ultimatum: he said that either he'd keep Debra and make sure that she was ready in nine months or he'd get rid of the mentoring programme which he'd spent a lot of time and energy fighting for.

Huh! He knew how much she spent on air travel last quarter alone and the mentoring programme was a bargain. Still, he had to admit that the whole premise could seem to come across as a bit "airy fairy". Not to mention, given his behaviour in the meeting with Sara, he probably wasn't the best advert for how EI can help you succeed in a matrix. And, given that was what the whole premise of the mentoring he was providing, Johann couldn't help feeling a bit worried.

How, he wondered, had he got himself into a situation where now, despite having a to-do list as long as his arm, he had to carve yet another hour out of his day to meet with this young, disaffected high-flyer? Normally Johann would have done a bit of research and been prepared with basic information and good questions, but he hadn't found the time. So, to some extent, he'd have to wing it.

Quickly skimming the notes in the performance management system he remembered what the Talent Manager in Debra's department had said: high potential and clearly not as engaged as she was last year. It was suspected that Debra was annoyed not to have been promoted but her manager had not had that conversation with her. Johann thought – so many problems could be solved if people would just step up and have that difficult conversation.

Not that he necessarily believed everything the Talent Manager, Yulia, was it?, said. He'd learned over the years that, even with no malice or deliberate attempt to mislead, important things get lost in translation and motives are ascribed where they don't exist. And, with HR, he thought with a smirk, you can never be sure that there isn't malice!

As he dismissed this uncharitable thought, there was a tentative knock at his door. He raised his voice:

"Come in!"

A head poked around the door. In her early 30s, Debra was well-dressed with a couple of quirky touches – Johann particularly noticed the enormous green ring on her right hand. Making eye contact she enquired:

"Johann?"

Johann smiled in return and nodded asking:

"Debra? Come in! Come in!"

Johann was moving around the desk as Debra approached.

She entered the office confidently and leaned forward to shake his hand. Johann was pleased – he always found it, despite himself, difficult to warm to someone with a limp or overly strong handshake and knew he wasn't alone in this having just the other day discussed it with some of his colleagues.

"Take a seat! Will you have a coffee? A tea?"

Debra asked if she might have a cappuccino and Johann called for his assistant to take the order.

"Two of your famous cappuccinos please Roshan."

Reflecting on how he found himself waiting for coffee to arrive with this woman who now had his reputation in her hands, Johann sighed.

He had pushed very hard to be given one day a week to devote to mentoring people from across the organization. The attendees had been chosen by a mixture of line manager nomination, HR approval and exec committee final signoff. Not that the signoff had been more than a rubber stamp. Until he'd made a fuss nobody had known about the programme. He'd been quietly getting on with it – seeing all of his mentees once a week – some just for a few minutes on occasion, and others for much longer. He should have kept it like that – off to the side. Less pressure. Ah, well. It was done now and he'd just have to make the most of it.

Anyway, he enjoyed the mentoring. It was fun to meet colleagues from across the organization, and he found that he often learned as much or more than he taught. But, even with the time he'd been given, it was difficult fitting in these sessions in addition to his "day job". Johann took it seriously and was constantly trying new approaches. He'd even joined a LinkedIn group and signed up for advanced training so that he could be a certified mentor and stay on top of any new research. Apart from anything else, and the management meeting debacle aside, he found that it made him better at his day job because he was more reflective – aware of what he was doing and the impact it was having so he could be more flexible and get better results. Not that it worked without fail. He sighed again. "I really must focus on keeping my temper or at least managing it better," Johann reminded himself.

Today was going to present more challenges than usual – he fully expected to meet some resistance to the idea of mentoring and coaching from Debra. On top of that, a couple of his regular mentees had dropped him a line outlining their objectives for the sessions or the issues that they wanted to discuss. There were some interesting conversations ahead!

 Key Takeaways

1. *Traditional training courses can work well in some respects, but in the end, most people simply revert to their standard way of behaving.*

2. *Many problems in the workplace could be solved if people felt more able to step up and have that difficult conversation.*

3. *Emotional intelligence may be the only tool beyond being skilled at your job that works.*

4. *It's possible to teach emotional intelligence by using it (and being transparent about it) during mentoring or coaching.*

2

Laying the Cards
on the Table

Roshan came back with the coffee and Johann, who had been making small talk, now turned his full attention to Debra's professional situation. Pulling his seat forward slightly, he gave his card to Debra who looked at it carefully before handing him her own. Pleasantries over, Johann got straight to business, admitting "I'm afraid I don't know as much about you as I would like as this has all happened rather quickly."

"Yes," said Debra.

Johann nodded as she stopped speaking. Although she was perfectly polite, did he detect a note of not exactly apathy but certainly a lack of enthusiasm? Maybe even hostility? He decided to probe a little further.

"So tell me a little bit about yourself and why you're here."

Debra took a deep breath. "Well, I'm 32 years old. I have an MBA. I've been promoted four times in six years and I moved to this company eight months ago when I was made an offer I couldn't refuse." She stopped. "It wasn't just the money although I won't lie the package was very attractive and, of course, it's a prestigious organization; but it was also the chance for growth and development that I was shown."

Johann took a chance, "And do you feel, now, that you made the right decision?"

The hesitation was obvious as Debra's mouth opened slightly.

Johann interjected: "I'm sorry. I should have been clear up front on confidentiality. Assuming you don't tell me anything illegal or against the company's rules, everything we say in here is completely confidential and I will share nothing without your express say so. That's one of the rules of the programme and I take it very seriously."

Debra's shoulders fell and she leaned forward. "To be honest, I'm not sure. I enjoy my work and I think I do a good job. In fact I know I do a good job but I've just been turned down for a job that I know I can do and been assigned a mentor!" Listening to her voice rise and the tension creep in, Johann prompted her.

"So it doesn't sound like you're very happy with the situation?"

"Would you be?!" Debra paused before starting again in a calmer voice: "I have already done the majority of that job. The only difference would really have been the size of the geography – I'd have been working across the whole region which really is the only next move for me if I'm going to stay here. And I don't want to leave – it's a great company, I like the people and the work . . ."

"And you've only been here eight months," Johann suggested.

"Quite," Debra agreed dryly. "Even in today's environment that could seem a bit flaky." She stopped, embarrassed that she had admitted considering this to someone so senior.

Johann just nodded his head. The internal recruiter had already flagged that he had received Debra's CV from a "recruitment consultant" who clearly wasn't doing his job properly if he thought it was ok to send resumes to current employers! "And the mentoring programme?"

Debra looked puzzled so Johann elaborated, "you said you know you do a good job but you've been turned down and given a mentor."

"Exactly. Again, I don't understand it. I get good performance reviews. I'm always level 4 or 5 or 'matching' or 'exceeding' expectations. I'm involved in a lot of cross-functional projects and now I'm being pulled away from my work. For what? I don't get it!"

Johann paraphrased, "So you feel like the mentoring programme is for people with performance issues and you don't believe that this description applies to you?"

"Exactly!"

"And nobody has discussed this with you?"

Debra shrugged, "Well, one of the guys from HR told me that there was a mentoring programme for people who need help to get to the next level and I was lucky enough to have been chosen."

Johann shook his head and smiled. "OK, let's try something. Think about these questions. What percentage of people in this company would like a promotion? And what percentage would need some help to get there? And what percentage does the company invest in time and energy and, let's be frank, money to the extent that they get to work with, and I say this with no false modesty, a very experienced and talented senior manager?"

Debra grinned as she noticed Johann dip his head and raise his hand as though to toast his own brilliance. "Fair point. I suppose you could look at it like that. I guess this is an investment in me."

"Exactly! We can see you are a high performer and we believe you have the potential to rise much further in the organization. We don't want to lose you but nor do we want to set you up to fail. In other words, the mentoring is not because we don't believe you can do the job, it is because we want to prepare you to succeed. This is not just because we're lovely people but because it makes economic sense for us to do so. It costs a lot of money to hire you, and we haven't got our return out of you yet! On top of that, we want to invest in you so that you're worth more to us. What do you think?"

Debra was still smiling. "Well, when you put it like that. But come on, let's be honest. I've heard this all before. There's always another training course to go on."

"Exactly. Look, I get it, but the worst-case scenario for you is that this is a 'fad' and we're just paying lip service and you'll waste a bit of time but you can always look for another job then." He looked at Debra. "Or maybe you'll find that it's useful. What have you got to lose? Looking at your last review you said that you felt that you hadn't got enough development opportunities. This is a development opportunity if you want it."

Debra thought for a moment. She couldn't see what was in it for him – why was he giving up his time for this? I suppose he could just be bored, she thought. She imagined he was probably making a nice amount of money, had a nice wife, a nice life – their kids were doing ok at school and they could afford to travel and buy nice things. Maybe he'd been doing the same job for ages and just wanted to "give something back". She stopped her eyes from rolling, aware that Johann was looking at her.

"OK," she said brightly, "how does it work then?"

"The idea is that we meet twice a month for about 60 minutes a time. How we use the time is up to you. We can work on particular skills you want to develop and, ideally, we'd work on something that was 'real'. For example if you want to improve your 'stage presence' in presentations or write better emails or develop your ability to influence others we can work on that. Whatever you want – we just have to be clear on what we are trying to achieve and why. From there we'll work out a plan and then implement it."

"Sounds great – I'd like to have someone I can trust to talk things over with. It seems like a lot of work for you though? Do you do this with others?" Debra was interested to find out how many other people were given this "special" opportunity.

"Yes, a few. It changes over time. People come and go and sometimes I know I'm going to be particularly busy – like last year when my grand-daughter was born I started to reduce the number of people I work with. But I missed it so here we are . . ."

Debra murmured "I see" as Johann pulled out a photo of a pretty little girl about 10 months old. "Beautiful," she said, smiling and, after a respectful pause, "So, tell me, when and where would we meet?"

"I like to devote a whole day every week – other mentors do it differently but I've found this to work best for me. You can have as much time as you like – first come, first served but the minimum is a 15-minute phone call and the default expectation is to meet for 60 minutes face to face. The most important thing I've found is to meet regularly and to stick to the meetings we agree. If we don't then it becomes difficult to maintain momentum."

Johann paused and smiled, "I should tell you one thing – I have a hard time with lateness as I read it as disrespectful, regardless of my best attempts to see it otherwise since I know it's not always the case. Anyway, work with my PA, Janet, to make it happen. She'll be in touch tomorrow to make sure you have all the necessary contact details. But the responsibility of making the appointment is yours." Johann looked directly at Debra as he spoke; he wanted her to understand that this was important.

Debra nodded agreement. She, too, struggled with people being late for meetings or work – she dreaded to think how much time the company was losing every year as a result of all these "small" delays. Maybe she could work with this guy after all.

"So we've covered why we're here (we want to keep you) and what we want to achieve (you being ready for the next step) and we've also dealt with some logistics – how often we'll meet, and how you'll set up the meetings."

Johann took a deep breath. He still found it difficult to state what seemed to be obvious to him but he knew, from experience, how much of a difference it made to be completely transparent where possible.

"I'd like to be up front about what I want to get out of the mentoring work we'll do and also about my concerns. I'd like to share them very honestly and hear your thoughts. My experience tells me that this helps to make sure the work we do is successful. Then I'd like to hear the same thing from you. Is that ok?"

Debra nodded again. This was more of the "airy fairy" approach she had been expecting from a "mentor."

"Great. So, obviously I'm a boring old man who has been everywhere and seen everything and am now wise and grey-bearded so this is a great opportunity for me to have a captive audience."

Johann trailed off as he realized that Debra wasn't entirely sure he was joking. He grinned. Although he was a grand-father he was still a young man at 55. Wasn't he? The grin faded.

"Joke! Although you should be clear that there are, in fact, some substantial potential rewards for me in mentoring you – Sun Microsystems compared the career progress of about 1000 employees over a five-year period and found that mentors were six times more likely to have been promoted and both mentors and mentees were about 20 per cent more likely to get a raise compared to others not in the programme.

"And the skills I've learned as a mentor have been really useful in my current day job too. So many of us come into management and we don't get enough training, or it's at the wrong time, or we've got a boss or a rewards system that forces us to create bad habits so that we aren't the best man-agers we could be."

Debra nodded, recognizing a number of the managers she'd dealt with.

"The mentoring training helped me to formally look at what I do and about how to get better. Really simple things that made a real difference.

"And, of course, there is the increased job and personal satisfaction – the rewards of seeing someone you've helped progress and succeed are probably the best thing.

"You know, I have been around the block a bit and learned some things and it's very rewarding to have a chance to share what little I do know."

Johann felt he'd gone on too long.

"But it's not just about what I know, it's also about helping you to develop in other ways and we need to work out what those are! So what about you? What do you want to get out of the work we do together? From me? How can I help you?"

Debra leaned back in her chair and took a sip of coffee. Johann seemed nice but she had had her fingers burned before. She decided to be as up front as he was.

"What I don't get," she sipped again, "is why the company is putting, as you said, so much time and energy into this mentoring thing?"

"Because it works!" Johann looked genuinely excited now as he leaned forward, his hands gesticulating.

"Organizations that continuously support mentoring achieve amazing results: they report increased retention rates, improved morale, increased job satisfaction and commitment, accelerated leadership development, better succession planning, reduced stress and stronger, more cohesive teams. We want some of that and we've found that, if we work at it, we can get it."

"OK," Debra was convinced that Johann, at least, really believed what he was saying but she still struggled. "So, really, how does this whole thing work?"

"It's almost like there must be more to it than just we meet and talk about stuff and things change as a result, right? And of course there is except, at the same time, there isn't!"

Debra looked more perplexed now than when she'd asked the question.

"Let me try again. It's like this. You have something you want to do better and the time we have together is time to get help on how to do that, then you and I go away and do the things we've agreed would help, then we meet again, see how it went, make any adjustments and, when we're happy, we move onto the next issue we'd like to tackle."

"That sounds easy." Debra relaxed.

23

"Exactly. You can use me as a safe place where you can try out new ideas and see how they fit. We can try to spot problems before they arrive and prepare for them. We can celebrate achievements and learn from setbacks and then, when you're bored with me and have wrung all you can from me, you will just up and leave!"

Debra was startled. She looked at Johann carefully. Relieved she started to laugh – clearly, Johann's sense of humour would need some getting used to.

"In the meantime, my job is to challenge you to think about what you really want, what new things you need to do to get them, new ways to think about things and to do things. We can talk about whatever you want and, if you need help in an area I don't know about I'll happily help you find someone who can sort you out. In my experience most of the issues are around people and what are called 'soft' skills but I'm interested to hear what you'd like to work on. Hit me!"

What do I have to lose? Debra thought. "Well OK. I suppose, off the top of my head, I'd like to work out why I didn't get the promotion and work on my issues related to that. Or the issues I'm perceived to have at least!"

"Great. And remember that these objectives can change. Once we've done something we'll re-evaluate and see what we want to work on next. OK? So let's say that in the subsequent session we're going to work out what stopped these people from giving you, so obviously qualified and clearly brilliant, this job which you could do with two hands tied behind your back!" Johann grinned at Debra. "So how are we going to do that? Where can you get information about why you didn't get the job?"

"Er, I guess I have the feedback from HR. And my own opinions of course."

"Both great sources of information. Where else can you get information on how you might be perceived? And the impact this has on you? And people around you?"

"I did a 360 a couple of years ago but that was in a different company . . ."

"It might be useful though if it's the only thing you've got. Anything else?"

"There's the performance review I had a couple of months back."

"Perfect. Anything else? Any psychometric tools or coaching reports for example? An assessment centre maybe?"

Debra agreed that she did have a rather old report from a psychometric assessment that she was prepared to share. The rest of the session was spent in logistics and small talk as they started to get to know each other better and they agreed that Janet would be in touch the next day. Just before she left, however, as she was shaking hands with Johann, he asked Debra one last question that was to give her food for thought over the next day . . .

 Key Takeaways

1. *Organizations that continuously support mentoring tend to achieve increased retention rates, improved morale, job satisfaction and commitment, accelerated leadership development, reduced stress and stronger, more cohesive teams.*

2. *Being mentored doesn't mean "you need to do your job better," but instead is to help prepare you to succeed.*

3. *Mentoring challenges you to think about what you really want and what new things you need to do to get them.*

4. *Mentoring has rewards for all involved.*

5. *Mentoring works but it takes dedication (time!) and hard work from all parties.*

3

Preparing for
Change

The next day Debra was surprised to see an email from Janet in her inbox when she checked it at 8 am. Clearly Johann didn't let the grass grow. Despite herself, Debra was pleased that someone so senior made her such a priority and decided to respond immediately asking for an hour on the next "mentoring open day". This was what Johann called his weekly day devoted to working with or for his mentees and the next one was in six days.

She wasn't at all surprised when only three minutes later Janet sent her a meeting invite, with full, detailed instructions, for 11 am on Thursday, 3rd July. Janet also reminded her to send the documents she'd discussed with Johann, which she duly did, after she found them scattered through her hard drive. She really did need to get her filing sorted out but, for now, settled on just opening a nice new folder labelled "Mentoring" on her desk top. Into this she put the feedback from the 360 she did a couple of years ago. She remembered the occasion – a hideous "team-building" event where everyone gave the nicest possible feedback they could get away with and solemnly pledged to being "better" or to "get disciplined" or "move to great". Of course, she hadn't opened the feedback since and could hardly remember what it had to say.

Reading it now and against her better judgement, Debra was still pleased to read that she came across as "confident" and "straight-forward" and "not afraid to go the extra mile". She frowned slightly as she read on to the less positive comments and noticed, "Debra would do well to spend as much time thinking about what other people want as she does about her own position before she starts negotiation." She also grimaced at "I don't feel like Debra is always on the same side as me."

Remembering who said this she snorted but then a phrase from the meeting with Elena in HR where she got feedback on why she didn't get the promotion popped, unbidden, into her head. Elena had been talking about the need, in the new role, to work with a lot of functional heads, at the same level, and influence them to behave in new ways. There had been a "concern," she said, that Debra didn't always "synthesize" ideas.

Debra snorted again. She had had to ask for an explanation – apparently "synthesize" means "go to each and every person who could possibly care, carefully explain the situation to them, get their feedback and go around and around ad nauseam until everyone feels 'consulted' and has been 'bought in'." Well, they're right – I've real work to do and don't have time to waste on people who can't be bothered to read their emails or check the project details, she said to herself. It had been suggested that she consider a negotiation skills course, which she had agreed to do.

Next she looked at her latest performance review. To be honest, there wasn't much in it: she hadn't been at the company for very long and, in any case, few people at work seemed to take them very seriously. One of Debra's colleagues had mentioned, quite casually, that he'd had the same objectives for the last three years so that all he had to do every year was change the date and get the form signed. Debra remember turning to him quickly to check whether he was joking and noticing that everyone else seemed to take this as normal. On reflection she supposed that it hadn't been much different at her previous firm except that everyone pretended to take it seriously.

Finally she looked at one of those psychometric tests she had done even longer ago. This test was something called LIFO® that the FTSE 500 company she had worked with used in a number of different ways.

She had been offered it when she was made redundant and had found it useful then but hadn't given it much thought since. She was interested to see if the insights were still true. If she remembered correctly, it purported to identify basic characteristics that need to be accentuated or muted if you wanted to achieve different results with different people. She opened the report. Scrolling past the "blurb" she came to the main page of the report explaining where she sat on four distinct styles and the different drivers and motivations that generated her behaviour. It made sense to her and she could immediately think of examples of her behaving exactly as predicted by the LIFO® report. Shrugging as she closed the document, Debra wondered what difference knowing these things could make before remembering that she needed to get moving if she were to be on time.

Having looked at all the documents she was sending to Johann to help them both think about how she wanted to use her mentoring sessions Debra then sat with a pen and paper (sometimes the old ways are the best!) and asked herself the question Johann had suggested just before she left their first meeting.

"If you get stuck," he had said, "ask yourself this question: 'can I think of a time when I didn't get what I want out of a situation, whether at work or at home, no matter whether it was my fault or not? Where I wished things had gone differently?' If you are not some kind of super-human you will definitely be able to! Then write down the first one that comes into your head. Then the second. And keep writing. Aim for at least 15. They can be something that happened 10 years ago, or even longer, or it might be something that happens on the way home today. Don't censor them or worry about them being too trivial or too personal – you don't have to share them."

Debra started to write.

4

Working on Objectives

Debra found that she was looking forward to seeing Johann, her mentor (it still sounded strange to her ears), again. She felt that she had prepared well and was excited to get help on fixing the things that were stopping her from getting the job she wanted next.

Johann, too, was excited about his day. His mentoring days were the ones he most looked forward to. Although often the problems didn't have just one "right" answer and were mostly messy, "human" problems, he enjoyed helping his mentees navigate the workplace and get results. He had been pleased to see that Debra had asked for an hour and had provided him with her documents. He'd found time to look through and make some notes but, although he had a number of thoughts, he was aware of the need not to have too many pre-conceived notions and to let the mentee decide on the direction. As long as, of course, the objectives were work related and within the agreed parameters.

There was a knock on the door and Debra poked her head through, "still ok to meet?" Johann stood up and moved around the desk to greet her warmly. They sat and made small talk until Johann suggested they get to work. "I've had a chance to look at the documents. I thought they were interesting. What were your thoughts?"

As they discussed the documents Johann challenged Debra to see if she felt any of the "critical" comments could, if true, explain why she didn't get the job (the reason they were meeting today).

"I don't know, I don't think so."

"OK. So just in the context of you not getting the promotion for now, given the feedback you had from HR – if you look at the two of them together do you see anything?" Johann asked.

Debra remembered the comment she had dismissed and a positive comment about being straightforward – "maybe the hiring manager was afraid that I'd cause too much trouble?"

"OK. Was he right? Would you have done?"

Debra laughed. "I can see how he might have thought that given some things I did in the dim and distant past, but I really have learned a lot and had a detailed plan of attack – I mean I really had worked out exactly how to fix the problems of that department."

"Great. What didn't he like about the plan?"

"I never told him what it was. . ."

"Why not?"

Debra smiled ruefully. "He never asked?"

"Hmmm. OK. Any more? As you look over all the comments about you in these documents and, most importantly, think about them in the context of the list of situations in which you didn't get what you want, do you see any themes? Are people saying the same thing in different ways and with different examples?"

Over the next few minutes Debra looked at the comments and started to identify some themes. For example "Debra doesn't always give enough attention to the things that can't be explained in a spreadsheet" and "Debra needs to 'synthesize her ideas'" could, in some lights, be seen as the same thing. "And could be something that stops me getting what I want," she thought.

Noticing that she had identified a number of themes Johann interrupted. "That's great. Don't worry about them being fair or even relevant to you. In fact, forget that these 'themes' apply to you and just imagine that a candidate – another person – showed some or all of them. Could you imagine how they might make a recruiting manager think twice?

Debra considered. "Sure," she said. "Of course."

"OK. So here's the hard part. Look at the list and choose the things that you most believe apply to you." Johann paused as Debra did this.

"Might any of these explain some reluctance to give you the role you wanted?"

"Ouch. I preferred thinking that it was all somebody else's fault I didn't get the job!" Debra laughed but Johann was guessing that a little part of that statement was true.

"Maybe, let's think about that. Sometimes it is someone else's fault. But it's very hard to change other people – look how hard it is to change ourselves! It might also be that the other guy is out to get us. And this is sometimes true but it's mostly not the case. More often it's a mixture of several different factors and the only thing we can really control is ourselves!"

Johann brought the conversation back to the objective Debra had set for the first session – to think about what she wanted to work on so that she would get the next job she went for. Asking a number of different questions rapidly to keep the session high-paced and to put Debra under some pressure he continued.

"For now, let's assume that the people making the hiring decision were paragons of all the virtues and wanted nothing more than to find the right person for the job regardless of any other factors. If these super-human beings still decided not to give it to you, what might have been their reasons? What might they have been worried about? Concerned about? Freaked out about?"

"I guess I'd be most worried about my ability to work across different geographies."

"Why? What makes it hard to work across different geographies?"

"Well, you can't see people so it's harder to know what's going on. And to get to know them. You don't know what they care about and how to handle them. You may not understand some of the cultural issues I suppose . . ."

"OK. Great. So you have a clear understanding of the issues. How did you address these in your CV and interview?"

"Well, I suppose I didn't. And I don't know why – I absolutely have experience of dealing with all of those things successfully!"

41

Debra and Johann looked at each other.

"Could we spend a few minutes thinking about other things that might have concerned them and whether or not I addressed them?" Debra asked.

When they had finished Johann asked Debra to look at the list of situations where she had not got the results she wanted and asked her to identify any trends in her own behaviour. After a little while, Debra looked up.

"I think the 'not thinking enough about the other person' comes up again and again, for example when trying to get people to do what I want. I try to do it but under stress that good intent disappears and as a result I don't get what I want. And I don't think I am at my best in ambiguous situations. You know, where it's not clear who does what, when and for whom?"

Johann nodded. "Interesting. You didn't know this, of course, but you have just spoken directly to my theory that a lot of the problems we face come from working in a matrix environment. Almost all of the people I see have matrix problems. Of course these exist in any complex environment and the matrix is certainly one of those. And, of course, not every individual or, indeed, organization will have all of these problems but if the following things sound familiar I'll lay money that you work in a matrix organization!

"Does any of this sound familiar? Because you work across functions and geographies you interact with people who have different values, attitudes and expectations. There are crazy amounts of information you can't possibly keep up with because you seem to have to be involved in everything and not just what your job description might suggest. You don't know why you have to attend two of your regular meetings and there are many more where the presence of at least one other person in the room is a complete mystery. You are pulled in two or more directions and sometimes you seem to have completely contradictory objectives or targets. You, and many of your colleagues, aren't clear on exactly what their job is and where to go to get something done or approved. Decisions can take months to get approved by all the 'necessary' people.

"The matrix often brings multiple and complex reporting lines, confusion over accountability, competing geographical and functional targets, lack of clearly defined roles, too many people involved in the decision-making process, lack of support from senior managers, and the politics and conflicts arising from continual organizational restructuring.

"Poorly defined management roles lead to turf wars or lack of accountability, which means everyone is too busy playing games internally to win externally. There's room to 'slip between the cracks' – if a person wants to take advantage of

43

any confusion over managing performance, or if they can't make the necessary transition to self-management.

"In other words it's a disaster and then, to make it worse, we call the only skills likely to make it work 'soft' skills and don't consistently make helping people to get better at these part of all managers' (even the most senior) jobs!"

Johann took a breath. "Sorry," he grinned. "I guess there's nothing like the passion of a convert! I've been fascinated by this stuff ever since I read this article by Mayer and Salovey on emotional intelligence and I get a little carried away sometimes. Let's look at your LIFO® report before we finish up."

Debra explained the instrument to Johann who had never seen it before and, as she talked him through what it said about her, he encouraged her to give specific examples of when she had displayed the behaviours described.

As she finished, he interjected: "It's all very interesting. So, thinking back to our objective today, what are your thoughts now on why you didn't get the job? Apart from the panel being out to get you of course!?"

Debra smiled. "Look, I still think politics is important. Who you know and all that."

"Agreed. And that's never going to go away and we should talk about that again but, for now, let's say that's a percentage of the reason you didn't get the job – how big a percentage would it be? At most?"

"Forty per cent," she guessed.

"OK. So let's say that's true, would it be worthwhile spending time on the 60 per cent that we know we can change and leaving the 40 per cent for the moment?"

"Yes," Debra nodded.

"So to sum up, what do you think now were the most important reasons you didn't get the job?"

"They might have not known some of the great things I've done because I like to talk about the team and not get involved in playing politics or blowing my own trumpet. They might think I'm too focused on the results and am not afraid to knock a few heads together or upset people to get where and what I want."

Johann smiled. "With your permission, I'd like to share my thoughts so far. Would that be OK?" He paused to acknowledge her agreement.

"I agree with everything you say and I believe that improving your emotional intelligence would go a long way in helping you to do what you need to so that you are comfortable taking credit and can effectively use the tools available to convince, negotiate and, dare I say it, 'sell' to other people – whether it's selling you for a new role or a client on a new product or process.

"These are just my thoughts and, please do bear in mind that I believe, with the passion of a convert, that the matrix either creates or exacerbates a lot of the stress and strange behaviours that we experience in the workplace. I think that 'soft' skills are the most important set of skills to develop and strengthen for surviving and even thriving in the matrix. These soft skills are the behaviours that 'hang off' the four 'branches' of EI or emotional intelligence and so I think it's essential to work on emotional intelligence as part of any of the work we do."

Johann paused as he felt he'd noticed Debra's face tighten. "You aren't convinced?" he guessed.

Debra was surprised. She prided herself on her blank demeanour. "I suppose I am surprised to hear a senior manager talk about emotions. I was always taught business was about the bottom line. And the bottom line for me is getting that promotion so I'd like to focus on that."

"OK. I agree. In essence, what you're saying is that you want to get promoted – you're not into this 'soft' stuff? Is that right?"

Debra nodded.

"My point is, in order to do that, to make sure we have the skills and are seen to have the skills of leadership, we need to improve our emotional intelligence. But look, we are out of time, I tell you what – as I've said before you get to decide what these sessions will be about and I guarantee you that we'll work on whatever you want next session – either the things we noted down earlier or any new ideas that come to you as you 'percolate'. I hope that you found today useful at least?"

Debra agreed that the session had helped her get clarity on her role in not getting the promotion and consequently some things she'd like to work on.

Johann continued, "One thing really would help and that's if you could be as specific as possible in what you want to work on and why. By 'why' I mean 'why is this important to you?' and 'why do you think you need to work on it – how do you know there's a gap between where you are and where you want to be?'. I'd also like you to spend some time thinking about EI or emotional intelligence before the next session. Have a bit of a Google and read a couple of articles that I'm going to have Janet send you and if after that you don't want to spend time on EI then that is absolutely fine with me." Johann's voice rose at the end of the sentence as he sought and got acceptance from Debra for this idea.

Smiling, Johann got up and shook Debra's hand warmly as he walked her to the door.

"Looking forward to seeing you soon – give me a call if there's anything urgent in the meantime!"

He turned and, sitting down, quickly made a few notes, in particular covering what Debra had identified as the areas she wanted to work on. He realized that they hadn't moved forward in solving any of the issues she had identified yet but felt that the time spent helping Debra come to her own conclusions on what these were was time well spent. She was now engaged with the process and motivated to make some changes.

It was a little disappointing she didn't seem too interested in building her emotional intelligence but he knew from past experience that, as the poet said, "a man convinced against his will is of the same opinion still," so he was prepared to wait.

Johann turned his attention to his screen again and confirmed that his next mentee should be waiting outside. Sure enough, there was a knock on the door. "Karim," Johann said as, once again, he moved from behind his desk.

 Key Takeaways

1. *When something goes wrong or we don't get what we want, it's usually at least somewhat our fault. In any case, that's usually the only bit we can work on.*

2. *Starting from the other person's point of view is always instructive – it helps you understand what might be concerning them. You can then check this and address it.*

3. *Many of the things that you may find stressful are likely to come as a result of working in a complex environment like a matrix.*

4. *Just relying on positional power ("I'm the boss") doesn't work where the lines of authority are blurred, i.e. anywhere you have cross-functional teams or more than one reporting manager.*

5. *Not having clarity is part of working in a complex environment.*

6. *This complexity isn't going away so either you change or you carry on with the stress.*

7. *You can't always hide your reactions – even when you're trying to.*

5

How Quickly
We Forget

Debra walked back to her own office. She'd made some notes during the session and re-read them slowly. Then she opened her computer and searched for "Emotional Intelligence". Following links that seemed interesting she spent about an hour researching the term and, at the end, had more questions than she did answers. There certainly seemed to be a lot of talk about it but she wasn't sure she really had a handle of what it was or how one would go about developing it: the training courses she had looked at seemed a bit vague and "woolly".

She also read some of the articles and links Johann had sent – it seemed that Johann's theory about the matrix had some basis in the research and a mass of people seemed to agree with him. Debra wondered why a structure that caused or exacerbated so many problems would ever be put in place. She was looking forward to hearing Johann answer that one!

The phone rang and, before she knew it, Debra was back in her normal routine and her session with Johann only came to mind occasionally over the next few days.

6

The Matrix – the Good, the Bad and the Ugly

D ebra was not in a good mood as she entered Johann's office for their third meeting. One of her colleagues had just been promoted and, although the guy who got it was good, she didn't think he was any better than her. Well, except at one thing, he was always playing politics – sucking up to the more senior guys and volunteering to be on any committee going.

Debra knew the type – went to the same school, belonged to the same club – she didn't have a hope against the kind of connections he had so she might as well give up. It seemed doing a good job just wasn't enough around here. This was exactly what she said to Johann when, after a few minutes settling in, he asked her how to elaborate on her comment of "I've had better days".

Johann nodded. "So you feel that, no matter what, this guy was always going to get the promotion because he is well connected and sucks up to those who can help him? And there's nothing you can do about it?"

Debra indicated her agreement. Johann went on "OK. I think you have managed to tell yourself the three 'clever stories' identified by those guys who wrote that *New York Times* bestseller *Crucial Conversations*, and I'd like to try to ask you some questions that might help you change perspective. The first one is 'why would a good person do something like that?' or, to put it another way, if you look at the behaviour of your peer when he's 'sucking up' can you come up with any other explanation for his behaviour?"

Debra thought for a moment. "I suppose he could just be ambitious and very interested in his field."

Johann added, "Yes. Or he could be in a horrible marriage and wanting to spend as much time as possible at work."

Debra raised her eyebrows.

"Or he could be under enormous pressure to support three families. Or he could be a suck up of course. The point is we have no way of knowing. Assuming the worst of him doesn't help us work with him. Or think about our part in the situation. Let's try the same question again but, this time, thinking about the hiring managers. Again, assuming they are 'good people,' why would senior managers hire anyone other than the most competent?"

"Maybe they're incompetent themselves?" suggested Debra.

Johann smiled. "Absolutely. That's certainly an option. There must be others though?"

"I suppose it is hard to hire people and they can only work on what they know – if they see him performing well and trust him because of their personal connection then I guess it makes sense to go with him."

"Great. OK. How about this question: 'what are you not noticing about your role in this situation?'"

Debra reflected. "I suppose I'm back to what we discussed last time – hiding my light under a bushel. I mean, I doubt if any of the people on the hiring committee had even heard of me before the interview process."

Johann then asked the final question he had learned to help with the three "clever stories" of victim, villain and helplessness. "What can you do now to move towards what you really want?"

"Well, I suppose what I really want is to get the recognition I deserve without feeling like I'm stepping over other people."

Johann leant forward, "And what's stopping you doing that now?"

"Nothing, I suppose. It just feels a bit, well, 'slimy'."

"OK. Try thinking about it like this – you don't have to be nice to people you don't like or think about yourself constantly. Instead you have to find something interesting or admirable about everyone that you can and constantly be looking for ways to help others – at any level of the organization. Does that still sound slimy?"

Debra agreed that it didn't and began to sketch out a number of things she could do to improve her profile and reputation in the organization including volunteering for high-profile projects and addressing networking groups and presenting at conferences.

Johann was pleased but, aware that "the road to hell is paved with good intentions" he pushed hard – getting Debra to put in the detail of what, exactly, she was going to do by when and whose help she would need. As her mentor he offered to make a couple of introductions and to work with her on the first presentation.

"Great," he said. "We've got our first set of actions – let's just confirm that they are SMART before we move on."

Debra was surprised that such a senior manager was prepared to get into such detail and, noticing this, Johann explained that experience suggested that the couple of minutes spent ensuring the actions to be taken were clearly understood and specific, measurable, achievable, relevant and time-bound was worth it in the end as people were more likely to do them.

"So," he continued. "Did you have a chance to look at the information I sent you? What are your thoughts?"

"Yes, thanks," Debra replied. "They were very interesting. I suppose my first thought is really a question: everything I read seemed to imply that the matrix presents enormous challenges and, when I look at my own situation that rings true, so I can't really understand why an organization would decide to put a matrix structure in place."

Johann smiled. "I know what you mean. Working in a matrix is hard but companies often have good reasons to decide on it anyway. To help us work out what they might be – let's define a matrix organization. OK?"

Debra thought before replying. "As I see it, a matrix organization is one where you have more than one person relying on you or, I suppose, where you rely on more than one person. If the person or people you report to day to day are different from the person who you report to on a more formal basis and who directly signs off on your performance review, salary and bonus then you're in a matrix. There are different 'flows' of authority – horizontal and vertical – across, for example, geographies, skills and industry."

She continued: "When you say it out loud like that, it's obvious that would create problems – people don't know where the power lies so they don't know the right thing to do. As a result they are going to waste huge amounts of time going from pillar to post checking in on everyone and getting consensus, or they will go maverick and play only by their own rules or they'll give up. And if you give up in the matrix it's very easy to slip between the cracks as you can play one side off against the other and, mostly, avoid being held accountable!"

"Wow. That seems very bleak. You've spent most of your career working in a matrix organization, right? What might be the pluses of working in a matrix? And have you never seen anyone who managed to get things done effectively and without becoming 'that guy?' Sorry that's two questions. Let's take the first one. What might be the pluses of working in a matrix?"

"Assuming a perfect world?" mused Debra. "I suppose it gives me the chance to work on different projects with people from different backgrounds and so learn a lot. In theory I can see a number of different career paths because I've had an opportunity to specialize but also to move up within that specialization and gain other skills by moving geography. I've never been bored at work because there's always a new project to get you out of your routine.

"From a personal perspective the benefit should be that you have a wider network and so the ability to learn, progress and move elsewhere in the world – if my functional boss believes I should be promoted I have 80 countries to look at but if my geographical boss says the same thing then I have to take his job!

"The matrix is a network of knowledge and exposure. It allows sharing of knowledge and can give great intercultural competence as the influences from all sides are visible and you are exposed to different cultural approaches.

"It's also more complex work because you have different stakeholders bringing in views and expectations and you need to find a way to meet best the business expectations but then also work out how to satisfy all the stakeholders. The projects and work can become very challenging and interesting and you have opportunities to be creative. We have to win people over to ideas to promote a good solution. And you get exposure to multiple styles of leadership or at least management one level above you so you can learn from different approaches and styles."

"Yes," said Johann. "I know that I've personally moved from specialist to generalist roles in a way that was made easier by working in a matrix. I worked on one project that involved me collaborating and having to persuade a group of different country managers, all of whom had better things to do with their time like their day job, to adopt a new process when half of them didn't even understand why we needed a process at all. I learned a lot about the importance of knowing how to sell ideas and negotiation at that time! I also learned about the need to make the connections and build the relationships before you start knocking on people's doors. It's like when you're a teenager and there were people who you knew to be 'users' and you didn't like or trust them. That hasn't changed – we just call it something else or don't mention it at all now. But we still notice!"

Debra was surprised to hear Johann mention something that seemed so personal – she guessed that he hadn't always been so open and decided to ask but, before she could go on, Johann continued.

"Anyway, other good things about working in the matrix?"

"I can't believe I'm saying this as I've seen it work so often in the opposite way but, in theory, it should allow an entrepreneurial culture where there is flexibility: the flexibility to attend to multiple projects simultaneously and adapt the teams in a sort of 'Mix & Match' to get things done. It's like having those Lego® pieces and you take the ones you need and slot them into place but it's not permanent."

"Yes," said Johann. "In reality, of course, it sometimes works the other way and the flexibility is destroyed because of the time needed to get consensus. As you said before that's when we see the 'mavericks' go off and do side or pilot projects outside the matrix which, if they work, are then accepted in the wider organization. I often wonder if we shouldn't explicitly allow this as some other companies do rather than acting surprised every time it happens . . ."

Debra was interested in this idea but wanted to continue thinking about why the matrix might be chosen by organizations. She continued:

"I suppose there are times when there is no other way of doing things – in order to serve the client we need to have people from a lot of different backgrounds who wouldn't normally work together put in the same place but we still need to be able to manage them.

"And even your point about having to go around to all the stakeholders – OK, it takes time up front but I bet that, when that's done properly, and not just as a box-ticking exercise, anything that's adopted stays adopted over the long term. When experts from different fields get to really work together – when they have a platform where their voices can be heard and they do speak up, but from a position of knowing what the overall objectives are – their contribution is invaluable. That way we get better decisions and, because they belong to everyone, they actually get implemented."

"And from the point of view of leading a company? Can you see any advantages there?" Johann prompted Debra.

"Well, thinking about it from your point of view, I suppose it must help to have different versions of what is going on and what is important to help you make up your mind on any given decision. If Ahmed was in charge then we'd be entirely focused on stock levels and if it was Colin it would be all about the margin and to hell with quality or getting it to the clients!"

"Exactly, we should be able to get different perspectives – specialist and generalist – I mean, it was a great help to me when I took this role to be able to talk to my counterparts in other countries. There is a real benefit at the organizational level if you have the ability to debate from different perspectives. That's often a big 'if' of course as people often don't speak up. But, I know that if I hadn't had a functional boss outside of the region I'd have been more insular, wouldn't have learned so much and wouldn't have had the chances I have had."

"Yes," Debra resumed. "And I suppose the matrix should make it easier to build a global pool of talent that is easy to find because, by definition, there should be a map to any skill

I'm looking for. For example if I want a guy who specializes in selling widgets in Asia I should be able to find him."

"Which, in turn, should allow us to serve our client well because we can cater for specific needs." Johann finished her thought and smiled. "That's a lot of good things that the matrix should bring. Convinced?"

Debra considered. "I understand that. In theory, this is all true but the problems remain. They're not made up – we've all experienced them."

"Fair enough. The world isn't perfect. But let me go back to my question from earlier – have you ever seen anyone who managed the matrix and got the most out of it? Maybe it wasn't perfect – remember, sadly, the world isn't. But have you ever seen anyone who did it well?"

Debra conceded that she had: "Lots of people, sure."

"And what did those people have in common? How did they make the most out of the positives of the matrix? How did they manage it well?"

"Well, they were all really well connected, people liked them, you felt like they cared. . ."

Johann interrupted, "cared about what?"

"Good question. Cared about me and the project. The team and the results. They were always clear on what was wanted and expected and asked for that clarity if it wasn't there so that everyone knew what the objectives were and they spoke up when something wasn't right but in a way that didn't upset other people. They could prioritize properly."

"And how did they do that?"

"They built great relationships, they were trusted. So they could say the 'unsayable' and they knew what was going on so they could make good decisions."

"And how did they do that?"

There was silence. Debra didn't know the answer to that. How did someone become trusted? How do you build a great relationship?

Johann looked at his watch. "I'm afraid we're out of time. Why don't you take that as your 'homework' until our next session – to come up with some ideas about how people build relationships and trust?"

As they were shaking hands Debra thanked Johann for his time and acknowledged that she had some things to think about before their next meeting.

Key Takeaways

1. *We tell ourselves three clever stories that can undermine us, but we can use three questions to get past them. We then refocus on getting the results we want for ourselves and others.*

2. *Networking doesn't have to be slimy but it does involve meeting people and trying to understand them.*

3. *Make sure your objectives are SMART – you're more likely to achieve them and achieving them is your responsibility.*

4. *The matrix presents opportunities as well as challenges. You don't have control over all the resources you need and so have to influence them.*

5. *Relationships are key to building connections and understanding others. If you can't understand them, you can't change their mind. You need to spend time doing this.*

6. *Spend time building a consensus of understanding the problem to be solved. Without this, you have no hope of getting real "buy-in" for a project which means everybody, even those who still don't 100 per cent agree, does what it takes to make it a success.*

7. *Developing solutions may be the "fun" part, but without the previous two steps you will probably waste time in the long run.*

8. *If people don't trust that you care about them and the project, you won't get the best results. If they do, then a lot is possible.*

7

What do the Successes in the Matrix do?

Debra let out a deep breath. It had been a very long week at the office. Or, rather, mostly *not* at the office as she had been travelling throughout the region and so her normally well-pruned inbox had grown out of control. Despite that, she had promised herself one hour to sit and consider what it took to build good relationships and trust and to succeed in the matrix.

Reflecting on the people she trusted, in and outside of work, and the people she had seen build good relationships she realized that all of them were able to work well with others. She laughed as she thought back to Johann's comment about teenagers and realized that "playing nicely" or, as we call it now "team work," remained an important skill. She made sure her phone was off and started to write:

They . . .

- *do what they promise*
- *tell the truth*
- *try to help*

- *ask lots of questions*
- *show vulnerability*
- *listen and remember what you said*
- *learn fast*
- *think about others and what they need – up, down and across the organization and outside*
- *are open-minded*
- *can communicate well with different people and groups*
- *build their profile*

Debra paused – wow! Who can do all of that all of the time!?

She reflected that, although this list made them sound like "nice" people (and they often were, although none of them were perfect) they weren't pushovers.

Instead, they had worked out that the only way to get things done if you can't just order people to do it (and that very rarely works and even more rarely does it work for long or as well as the other options), is to influence them. And that influencing others means being able to see the other point of view (even if you don't agree with it) and understand their motivators and levers so that you can articulate things in a way that makes it clear what's in it for them.

The matrix is about getting things done even when you don't have any power, Debra continued to write. *And the ones who succeeded in it understand that and act accordingly.*

They don't assume they know everything – they keep up to date on the research and use this to help them get better at what they do. She thought of one guy she used to work with who used Robert Cialdini's research on influence to help him get a new benefits system accepted. Well, she conceded, he used a consultant who understood the research but at least he was open-minded enough to use the research!

Those successful in the matrix are all comfortable with change. Debra put her pen down and lost herself in thinking about the successes she had seen. They recognized change as a constant and weren't afraid of it because they had the tools to deal with it.

They know what battles to fight. And how to fight them. They understood the need to manage conflict to unsurface issues and the need to say things out loud to confirm their own understanding.

They know who they are and don't forget it – Debra remembered one leader she worked with who stood up to corporate HQ when they tried to enforce a global communication that he knew would be wrong for his team and, indeed, all the teams. Under pressure, he stood up for what was right and he had the relationships and track record to get it. Is that "authentic leadership" Debra wondered?

Debra considered something her father had said: "nothing happens until someone sells something to someone else. Especially if it's an idea". And the people she'd seen succeed knew how to do that. In other words, *they think about things from the point of view of others. And make sure their communications take these different perspectives into account.*

They recognize leadership in others, realizing it is not a function of title but rather an attitude and set of behaviours and they generously mentor and develop others. Debra reminded herself that they do this not only because they get something out of it personally but because it improves the resources (humans!) available to get things done.

They really understand the overall strategy and how what they and others do support this and they share that so that everyone sees how they contribute to the business. Debra reflected that this helps them to manage competing objectives and priorities – often one of the most important battles in the matrix.

They hold people to account – immediately and in a way that helped them rather than belittled or bewildered them. Debra thought about the people she saw failing in the matrix and realized how often she heard them use excuses like "well, I'm not their manager" to avoid holding people to the promises they made.

They believe that a real team means conflict and they encourage that. It's so natural to want to avoid conflict and to think that will help a relationship but when we don't get everyone's views upfront we make poorer decisions and it's difficult to get full commitment and so successful implementation on any decision made.

They listen and are aware that "in order to be understood, you must first understand". The successes spent time understanding the pressures others were under so they could help them where possible. Debra thought of a project leader she knew who always remembered the end of quarter nightmare for accounts and adjusted their meeting agenda to take this into consideration and give the finance team more time when they were under the most pressure.

They always think of others – remembering to connect people and help. Not because this is the "nice" thing to do but because it gets them results. Debra recalled a story an MBA class-mate of hers had told in defence of his role in internal communications which had been coming under some fire. The young man had explained that, because of his position, he travels extensively and so has informal conversations with people in various functions. More than once he had been able to identify individuals in the same function with the same problems but in different countries. He then helped them connect – often through the functional head. The help he provided to

77

others improved his relationship with them and made it easier for him to get things done.

This reminded Debra of a key behaviour for success in the matrix: *they understand that authority comes from personal relationships and so they make sure to spend time developing these.* When Debra reviewed the people she saw succeed in the matrix she realized that they put in the time in advance to build relationships and they stayed in touch. They weren't "users" who only got in touch when they needed something. And so they were remembered: when an interesting project or role came up, they were at least considered.

They lead by example and understand the power of symbolism. Debra thought about the new CEO she had heard of who had to impose strict cost-cutting throughout the organization. He made sure that he and all of his team never left a room without turning off the lights and the AC and ate with the rest of the workers in the canteen. Needless to say, everybody else joined in too. Of course that, on its own, wouldn't be enough but it sure sent a message.

They are open about their own needs. They can say that certain working styles are easier for them to deal with than others and they are clear about where their limits are. Debra admired this ability, most of all as she struggled with it every day.

They are flexible and able to react appropriately in different situations – although always themselves they adapt differently in different situations. This wasn't as easy as people thought – Debra reflected as she thought of one colleague who, although a great guy to have a coffee and chat with (clients liked him for this), didn't seem to understand that he had to behave differently when with clients in the boardroom. She was sure that this was limiting his career. She wondered if maybe he didn't know that it was important?

"Hmmm," Debra thought, rubbing her hand which now ached. "How could he not know that? Surely he can sense the atmosphere? Or maybe he can't? Maybe he's good at all the other things on that enormous list and this is just a blind-spot? Or maybe, like me with the ability to be open about my own needs, he knows it but doesn't know how to get better at it? Only needing to get better at one of these things would be pretty impressive," she conceded. "I can see why the matrix can be so stressful if you need to do all of these things!"

Debra continued to write. *Perhaps most important of all they recognize how important these skills are and so they spend time honing them and practising them.*

"Those who can behave like this have got it made, assuming they are technically skilled as well of course, because they can access all the information and resources they need, get

79

people behind an idea and really make an impact to the business," Debra thought. "But what if you're just not that kind of person? What if this stuff doesn't come naturally?"

She looked at her phone and, remembering that she had to be at the cinema at 9.30, Debra turned it on and started to get ready.

 Key Takeaways

1. *Think about others and what they need – up, down and across the organization and outside.*

2. *Aim to communicate well with different people and groups, by telling the truth, thinking from the perspectives of others, asking questions and listening!*

3. *Encourage conflict in a team, rather than avoiding it! Without it, you don't get everyone's views upfront, which makes it more difficult to get full commitment and successful implementation on any decision made.*

4. *The matrix is about getting things done even when you don't have any power. Personal relationships are the answer – so make the time to develop them.*

5. *Leadership is not a function of title but rather an attitude and set of behaviours.*

8

Defining EI

J ohann smiled as he watched Debra take a number of sheets of paper out of her bag.

"This is what I came up with when I sat down to think about what it takes to do well in the matrix. And then I Googled it for a while and there didn't seem to be anything hugely important that I had missed. What do you think?" She offered the papers to Johann.

"It's great to see you've put so much thought and work into it. Before I look at the list, let me ask you a couple of questions."

Debra nodded.

"OK. The first question is 'if you could do all of the things on your list perfectly would it solve all the issues created or exacerbated by working in a matrix?'"

Debra laughed. "I think it would solve most problems in the world! Seriously, let me look back at what we said the main problems were for people working in a matrix. We said that people in a matrix work across functions and geographies, with people with different values, attitudes and expectations. This means that communication can be difficult even if there is an apparently shared language. They often suffer from information overload as they are peripherally involved in a very high number of projects or initiatives and struggle to manage their time. As a result, their 'day job' suffers. Sometimes they have conflicting or what seem like completely contradictory objectives and targets. Decisions can take months to get approved as 'everyone' needs to consulted. As a result some people go maverick and play only by their own rules – which they'll probably get away with for a while as there may be confusion over who they are accountable to."

Johann grimaced, "succinctly put!"

"So yes, maybe. If I could, in some parallel universe, do all of the things on this enormous list, then I would probably be able to get over most of these problems."

Johann pushed further, "And would it allow you to take advantage of all the potential in the matrix?"

"You mean the chance to work on different projects with people from different backgrounds so that you have a wider network and so the ability to learn, progress and move – by function or geography for example? To be able to use the diverse experience and knowledge so that we get to the best possible solution? To be a clever Lego® piece who uses the flexibility of being able to do different things with different people so that I am aware of new opportunities and so that people think of me for these projects? To get to hear different points of views and expertise and use them to serve the client better so that we're all more successful? Yes," Debra admitted, "I think that I could really master the matrix if I could do the things on my list."

"OK. So, to sum up, we've identified the pros and cons of the matrix and noted down some things that people do to become successful in the matrix. Now we need to decide which ones you would like to work on." Johann paused again. "So which of these would you like to work on first?"

Debra looked down the list. Although she knew exactly what she should be working on – she had identified it as she wrote it down – she wasn't sure she should say it. Noticing her hesitation, Johann made it easier for her by asking a closed question.

"Do you know which one it is?"

"Yes," Debra admitted.

"What is it?"

"I don't want to say." The words escaped from Debra's mouth.

"OK. You don't have to say." Johann paused. "Why don't you want to say?"

"It feels very 'fuzzy' and self-indulgent. And I don't want to make you think that I'm either of those things."

Johann smiled again. "Would it help if I told you what I was working on with my coach at the moment?"

Debra was surprised to hear Johann had a coach. Clearly he really did buy into this development thing.

"We're working on my ability to prioritize – I've found myself overwhelmed as I've taken on new projects and I'm trying to get a handle on things. I've worked out that the criteria I used in the past don't work anymore, and I'm trying to come up with a new set."

"I want to work on being more open about my own needs." Debra spoke quickly.

"It seems like you've just made the first step!" They both laughed.

"The thing is," Debra continued, "everybody goes on about team work all the time and I want to be a team player – of course I do. I want to play nicely with others but I don't want to be a doormat. I'm fed up of working late because someone else didn't do what they should or seeing someone ruin a presentation I worked hard on. And they still get a good review and bonus and promotions."

"OK, well, leaving aside for the moment the whole question of teams and whether or not the current obsession with them is useful, let's try and focus on the real issue here. What are you trying to achieve? And remember it needs to be something specific so that we know if we've achieved it."

"I want to get better at saying what I want."

"Can you be more specific? Think about situations in which you don't say what you want and tell me what you want to change. Can you think of something that happened fairly recently maybe? Do you remember the details?"

"Well, actually, there was something this week. I have a colleague who is constantly late with reports. She always has a great excuse. But that's the point – she always has a great excuse. And it means I can't plan my own day with any kind of certainty."

"And you haven't spoken up? She doesn't know this?"

"She should know. It's obvious, isn't it?"

"Maybe. Although if it were obvious that would make her someone completely uncaring. Is she that person? In every situation?"

"Well, no. Not in every situation. In fact she was lovely to me when I first joined."

"What impact is her behaviour having on you?"

"It's stressing me out. And I try not to work with her now which is a shame because she'd be perfect for a project I want to run."

"So why don't you talk to her?"

"What's the point? She probably won't stop!"

"Well maybe not. But she certainly won't if you don't tell her, will she? Look, it's like this. Imagine you had a puppy and it peed in the corner. . ."

Debra looked at Johann, surprised. "OK" she said uncertainly.

"Bear with me. The first time the puppy pees it doesn't know any better, right?"

"Right."

"So, if you don't want the puppy to pee in the corner, you have to teach it that it's wrong, right?"

"Right."

"And if you don't teach the puppy then it's not the puppy's fault it misbehaves in the future, it's yours! Right?"

"Right."

Debra seemed to be following but Johann wanted to be sure. "What I'm saying is that your colleague is the puppy and you are not stopping her from peeing in the corner!"

Debra burst out laughing. "OK," Johann was laughing too. "Of course, I don't mean that she's a puppy or that you should train her like a puppy. I just mean that if you don't have the conversation nothing will change."

"OK, fair enough," Debra agreed. "But I don't know where to begin."

"Ah, well, that's a different problem," said Johann. "And I can help you with that. Here's a great book. Have a read of this and we can discuss it and use it to plan your conversation at our next meeting. OK?"

Debra took the copy of *Crucial Conversations* and, scanning the back briefly, put it in her bag and returned her attention to Johann.

"So," he said, "we talked about what you wanted to achieve and, in essence, it's about having the tools to have difficult conversations so that you can speak up without ruining relationships. As a first step towards getting there, you're going to read *Crucial Conversations* before our next session so we can then use it, if you want, to plan your conversation with the annoying colleague. Agreed?"

"Agreed," said Debra, wondering how she was going to fit this in on top of all the real work she had to do. Well, she could always just skim it.

"Is there anything that might stop you doing this? Do you have enough time? I don't want you to commit to something you can't do." Johann fell silent.

Debra looked at him. How had he known? "No," she said, "I'll read it and I'll be prepared. Thanks for the book."

"No problem." Johann crossed his arms. "So, we've looked at one thing on the list. You seemed to have a lot on there?"

Debra looked down at the sheets. "Yes, way more than is practical really. And, even more worrying, it all seems a bit, I don't know, 'nebulous,' is that the word? I mean, I've written that people who are good in a matrix are good at communicating. OK, fine. So what? I mean, how does it help me to know that? I suppose I could go on a communications skills course but, really, at this stage in my career? If I don't know by now how to look people in the eye and adjust my tone of voice then I doubt being told to do so by some over-priced trainer in a nice hotel whilst my real work piles up is going to help."

Johann was delighted that Debra was being so honest and straightforward – it made his life so much easier and, of course, it wasn't always the case with mentees. Or anyone for that matter.

"OK, well I can see how it's a bit overwhelming. In all honesty, I think that's why we tend to let the 'soft' stuff go – there's a lot of it and we don't seem to be very good at helping people to get better at it. That's why I think the idea of emotional intelligence is useful. It kind of provides a 'peg' on which all the different skills can be hung."

Debra didn't snort. She knew that wouldn't go down well and, although Johann talked about 'soft' skills, she definitely didn't want him to feel any disrespect from her as she wasn't sure that she wanted to be on his wrong side – he had a tendency to say things straight out that could be disconcerting.

And he asked good questions. In fact, he may have just asked one now. Debra pulled her attention back to the small room she was sitting in with Johann, who was looking at her expectantly. She shook her head. "Sorry, I was miles away. Can you repeat the question?"

Johann tried not to be irritated. "I asked if you felt whether you have a clear understanding of what is meant by EI or emotional intelligence?"

Debra considered: she had read all the articles Johann had sent her and she was sure that she could recognize someone who was emotionally intelligent but she didn't really have a definition. "No," she admitted, "I suppose I don't."

"I suppose it's no wonder we have such trouble selling the idea," Johann mused, "given nobody seems able to define it."

"That'll do for a start," thought Debra as she considered all the other objections she had to the idea of emotional intelligence.

"But, of course, there are a couple of definitions that are fairly well established and agreed. Having said that, I'm not sure that knowing a definition is as useful as getting the concept and living it – I remember a company I heard about that wanted to instil a culture where everyone spoke up. The way they did this was by putting everyone through training so that they could all define culture and identify cultural levers. It went really well – everybody could give the definition and tell you the seven levers or whatever.

Unfortunately they never did anything with those levers or the definition so the whole thing kind of died a death." Johann stopped talking.

"OK," said Debra, a little irritated herself now that Johann had started off on his talking horse again. "But it would be useful to see it defined and to *use*," she stressed the word, "that definition when we're talking."

"Fair enough." Johann fired up his computer. "I'll just be a minute," he said as he looked for the relevant file. Debra sat back and looked around his office. Noticing a picture of Johann and a very pretty blonde woman with two kids she asked, "is that your family?". "Yes," he replied, distracted, "my wife and our two grandchildren." Debra silently congratulated herself on not asking him if it was his daughter.

"Ah, there it is." Johann was triumphant. "According to my notes, Salovey and Mayer revised their initial definition of EI to: "The ability to perceive emotion, integrate emotion to facilitate thought, understand emotions and to regulate emotions to promote personal growth."

He stood up and wrote it on the whiteboard that covered almost all of one wall. "I'm not sure why they revised it – the old one seemed OK, and pretty much the same thing – academics! But what I like about it is that it is so simple. It says that emotional intelligence is about being able

93

to sense emotions and understand them so that we can use them when they're useful and manage them when they're not. What do you think?"

Debra thought it was a perfectly reasonable definition of emotional intelligence but she didn't know what she was supposed to do with it or how it helped her and she said this.

"Look, it's about behaviour really. What they're all saying is that our emotions impact our behaviour and so we need to be able to manage these if we're to manage our behaviour and get what we want.

And of course that other people's behaviour is motivated by their emotions and we need to be able to decode these, and help them to do so too, if we want to change their behaviour."

"That seems manipulative," thought Debra.

As if he'd heard her thoughts, Johann carried on. "Note that phrase 'help them do so too' – the idea is to use this for good although, like with any tool, people can use it to be manipulative. But I don't know what to tell you – that's true of everything, isn't it?" He shrugged his shoulders.

"Look, there's a lot of research out there (Goleman, Boyatzis and McKee's book springs to mind) that suggests that the 'leader's mood is quite literally contagious, spreading quickly and inexorably throughout the business'. They say that, because the brain's emotional centre, the limbic system, is an 'open-loop system' (it relies on external sources to maintain itself), then we rely on our connections with others to decide our moods. If our moods can affect others and theirs can affect ours then surely knowing that must be useful?" Johann stopped talking so that Debra could respond.

"OK, so emotional intelligence is about recognizing and using emotions so that we can manage our behaviour but there's got to be more to it than that?"

"Well, yes and no, I mean, Goleman's model looks at five different aspects of EI." He showed Debra a slide.

1. Self-awareness – the ability to know one's emotions, strengths, weaknesses, drives, values and goals and recognize their impact on others while using gut feelings to guide decisions.
2. Self-regulation – involves controlling or redirecting one's disruptive emotions and impulses and adapting to changing circumstances.
3. Social skill – managing relationships to move people in the desired direction.
4. Empathy – considering other people's feelings especially when making decisions.
5. Motivation – being driven to achieve for the sake of achievement

"That doesn't seem too far away from what the academics came up with? There's also an ability-based model done by Mayer and Salovey but I don't have much trouble seeing the similarities here too. This one looks at four types of abilities." He showed another slide on his screen. "Although, of course, the Goleman model talks about abilities underneath the five aspects I showed you before."

He paused. "This model sees emotions as information that helps you to make sense of the environment. And suggests that we vary in our ability to process this information and connect it to other things. That strikes me as true. What do you think?"

The ability-based model claims that EI includes four types of abilities:

1. Perceiving emotions – the ability to detect and decipher emotions in faces, pictures, voices and cultural artefacts – including the ability to identify one's own emotions. The first step in understanding emotions is to accurately perceive them. In many cases, this might involve understanding nonverbal signals such as body language and facial expressions which may differ across time and geography.
2. Using emotions – the ability to harness emotions to facilitate various cognitive activities, such as thinking and problem solving. Emotions help prioritize what we pay attention and react to; we respond emotionally to things that garner our attention. The emotionally intelligent person can capitalize fully upon his or her changing moods in order to best fit the task at hand.

3. Understanding emotions – the ability to comprehend emotion language and to appreciate complicated relationships among emotions. For example, understanding emotions encompasses the ability to be sensitive to slight variations between emotions, and the ability to recognize and describe how emotions evolve over time. The emotions that we perceive can carry a wide variety of meanings. If someone is expressing angry emotions, the observer must interpret the cause of their anger and what it might mean. For example, if your boss is acting angry, it might mean that he is dissatisfied with your work; or it could be because he got a speeding ticket on his way to work or that something you do reminds him of an old colleague.

4. Managing emotions – the ability to regulate emotions in both ourselves and in others. Regulating emotions, responding appropriately and responding to the emotions of others are all important aspect of emotional management. Therefore, the emotionally intelligent person can harness emotions, even negative ones, and manage them to achieve intended goals.

Debra considered. "So what they're saying is that EI isn't about character or personality traits, for example shyness or extroversion or even about particular talents, for example being great at golf. Instead it's about a mental skill set – it might come more or less naturally but we all have the same 'number of dots' – we're just more or less practised at connecting them and then doing something with the picture."

"Exactly. Great analogy. It's about being able to figure out your own emotions and those of others, and then doing something useful with that information versus being sociable or warm or mean or nasty. And, even assuming you notice the 'dots,' that is the emotions, understanding the picture you've drawn with those dots can be hard – especially if that picture is different from something we're used to seeing. Like when we're working across cultures or if there is some other thing that makes it harder to understand someone else's picture, for example the experience of being a different sex or race." Johann looked at Debra for confirmation that she understood what he was trying to say.

"So, although the emotion may be universal (everyone gets happy or scared or angry) the triggers might be different and so too might be the way those emotions manifest themselves? Hmmm, suddenly, recognizing emotions is harder than it first seems." Debra admitted.

"Right," Johann continued, "because not only do you have to be aware that other people are having emotions, be convinced you need to look out for them and be skilled at noticing them even with the 'noise' in the signals, you also have to be monitoring your own emotions and behaviours and all of this is in constant interaction whilst you simultaneously carry on a conversation about, for example, where to allocate resources in the budget."

Debra smiled. "Or something important?"

Johann didn't miss a beat. "You'd think, right? Given all the actually important things on our collective plate that we would all be wonderfully focused so that our personal and, some might say, petty emotions wouldn't get a look in but, of course, when it's important our emotions are clearly going to be involved. Having said that, some of the most emotional debates I've ever seen have been around the allocation of car park spaces!"

"So, if emotions lead to behaviour then why do we pretend that emotions aren't important at work?" Debra asked. She was genuinely interested to hear Johann's insights – especially about colleagues at his level.

Johann shrugged. "I've asked myself this a lot. I don't think it's because we don't care or don't believe it. I mean, these are intelligent people who *know* that emotions lead to behaviour. One of my colleagues said to me the other day, 'you know it's weird – we accept in the movies and novels that emotions lead to behaviours and behaviours lead to results – why would we think it's any different in organizations?' And she was right – organizations are about getting results. But if we just focus on the results nothing changes – we need to go to the source of results – behaviour – and even beyond that to what leads to behaviour – emotions! And emotions are tricky because, although we all have them, they may, as you say, be triggered by different things and be expressed in different ways depending on a variety of factors. Your experience leads to your understanding of your emotions and those of other people. To return to the movie analogy – we understand that movie characters have different reactions to events than we would have because they've had different experiences but we forget that in the workplace and treat everybody as though they are the same as us.

"For me it's very simple. I want as much information as possible when making decisions – in any part of my life. My emotions and their impact on my behaviour are part of that information and so are the emotions and so behaviours of the people I interact with. I'm not perfect but I am getting better at noticing the first step. And I know what questions to ask now.

"Emotional intelligence isn't about having the 'right' emotions or dictating behaviour but rather being aware of and thinking about what emotions are going on, why, the impact the emotions might have and what you're going to do about it.

"For example, I had a new CEO earlier in my career – he had taken over from a particularly well-loved leader under somewhat dubious circumstances. Rather than just carrying on he made sure to acknowledge the emotions and deal with them upfront – I reckon he saved himself (and us) six months of gossip and political manoeuvring!

"But, often, there is an element of 'I didn't get to where I am today'. The guys at the top either didn't need help to become emotionally intelligent because they were naturally good at this stuff. As a result they don't see the need for helping others, or they don't think a training course will work for whatever reason. Or maybe they don't see the need for emotional intelligence because in the world they worked in it was less necessary. Sometimes they hold all of these views at the same time. For example, they say things like 'our people should know this stuff already – it's basic' and 'I don't think you can teach this stuff – it's too hard'. Amazing!

"Deep down I think it's a lack of understanding – they haven't had the chance to observe people with high emotional intelligence. And, of course, you can ignore it and you may very well succeed anyway – perhaps you are indispensable in some way – but your career journey will certainly take longer and be more stressful for you and the people around you."

Johann realized he'd been talking for a long time. "And on that note we're out of time." He stood up. "Don't forget to read the book and come prepared to practise the conversation with your tardy colleague. Plus, we can always talk more about emotional intelligence if you want."

With her mentor's words still ringing in her ears and her head still somewhat confused by this sudden trend to talk about emotions the whole time, Debra left the room. If emotions are so important why didn't we learn about this stuff in school?

 Key Takeaways

1. *Organizations are about getting results. But if we just focus on results, nothing changes.*

2. *We need to go to the* source *of results – behaviour – and even beyond that to what leads to behaviour – emotions.*

3. *The definition of emotional intelligence, according to Mayer and Salovey is: "The ability to perceive emotion, integrate emotion to facilitate thought, understand emotions and to regulate emotions to promote personal growth."*

4. *Emotions are information that helps us make sense of our environment, they impact our behaviour and so we need to manage them. People vary in their ability to perceive, understand and manage their emotions but we can all improve.*

5. *Emotional intelligence isn't about having the "right" emotions or dictating behaviour.*

6. *Rather, it's about being aware and thinking about what emotions are going on, and why, the impact the emotions might have and what you're going to do about it.*

9

A Short and (Emotionally) Intelligent Review

Debra was pleased to be home and on her sofa. She had promised herself an early night with the book Johann had lent her. She was still surprised (and a bit amused) that such a gruff, ex-army type was this convinced that, beyond the most junior level when proving technical ability was important, emotional intelligence was the answer to a successful and less stressful career in a matrix organization. She knew that he was a real believer and he had convinced her that emotions led to behaviour and so deserved notice. However, she wasn't sure how that solved any of the problems she had or was likely to have.

She opened up the first page. The more interesting questions, she thought, were "how is this useful, in practical terms" and "can it be taught?".

Debra laughed when she thought about the likely spectrum of emotional intelligence. "What if it was like spatial intelligence? Her lack of that was what she used to explain why she had failed her driving test eight times! Maybe we should be testing for emotional intelligence or, at least, the ability to learn it when we recruit? We could save a lot of trouble if it's that important? Is that even possible? I must remember to Google that."

Debra's eyes closed as she came to the final page of the book and that was all she knew until she woke, disorientated, in the dark three hours later.

10

Working Out How
EI Can Help

Johann didn't need too much emotional intelligence to spot that all wasn't well with Debra as the normally very well-presented 30-something year old burst into the room, hair akimbo and obviously flustered, her jacket collar askew and three minutes late.

"I'm so sorry I'm late," she panted. She sat down and fumbled with her bag, finding and turning off her phone, before patting down her hair and fixing her collar.

Johann waited until she was settled. "All OK?" he enquired.

"No, no it isn't. I've had it up to here." Debra indicated a level far above the top of her head.

"What happened?"

"I just can't keep having the same conversation, again and again." The colour rising in Debra's cheeks grew more apparent as she spoke. "Ali just gave me a really hard time because I wasn't at the last weekly meeting. I tried to explain that I needed to be at a very important client meeting with Viren but she wasn't having it. I mean, what am I expected to do? Tell my boss 'no?' I can just imagine Viren's face!"

Johann grinned. "Sorry," he said immediately. "I wasn't laughing at you. I was just thinking about the matrix and how this is such a typical example of the difficulties. Let me step out of 'mentoring mode' and make a guess? You have two different people you have to do things for – two 'bosses' in effect, who both tell you everything is 'high priority' and expect you to be completely up to date on, and totally devoted to, their latest thing without considering the impact on you and your ability to get things done, not to mention your 'work/life balance'." He made the hand gesture signifying air quotes as he finished the sentence.

"Amazing," Debra murmured with what could have been a soupcon of sarcasm. Or perhaps she was merely annoyed by Johann's apparent delight in, or at least lack of concern about, her predicament.

"And, for my next trick," Johann bowed his head slightly, "I'm going to further guess, based on what we discussed last time, that you haven't said anything to either of them but have silently fumed, thinking 'they should know this' and 'I'll do better at this when I'm charge?'"

Debra nodded. She did recognize herself, reluctantly, in Johann's description.

"Remember, not speaking up means that nothing changes. You're missing a great opportunity to help yourself and your colleagues at the same time. As well as demonstrate your leadership ability by fixing, or at least trying to fix, a problem even when you don't have any authority. By not speaking up you fall into the same habit of not having the difficult conversations, of ignoring things that annoy you about your bosses."

Debra didn't respond. She was thinking. After a few seconds silence, Johann asked: "So, *Crucial Conversations* then, what did you think?"

"I enjoyed it," she said. "I hadn't thought about a lot of the things in there and there were some great tools. Especially for having what you call difficult conversations. And I accept the need for them. The thing is . . ."

She stopped, unsure whether Johann wanted to hear her concerns. "Yes?" He prompted her.

"Well, it's not exactly brain surgery. I mean, the things they suggest aren't difficult. It seems like there should be more to it?"

Johann smiled. "Yes, I know what you mean. It's not difficult but it *is* hard. The way I think about it – it's like giving up smoking or not eating chocolate – it's not actually that difficult to do, mechanically at least. Just don't light up or open the bar! But it is hard because the behaviours are ingrained. They're tied to emotions. The only way to do it well is to practise. Practise breeds habits, and habits become unconscious behaviours. In that way you always have those tools at your disposal. But that takes time and the only way to get there is with practise – so to begin with let's start with planning your conversations with your tardy colleague and two 'bosses'."

Debra sat forward and pulled her notes together. "One other thought," said Johann, "reducing your stress now might just help you in the future in a way that you hadn't considered."

Debra raised her eyebrows.

"According to the very latest research – in primates, OK, but there are reasons to think the results will be similar in humans – it seems that chronic stress over time depletes serotonin levels (serotonin of course affects moods or emotions) and so leads to more spiteful decisions. Maybe by speaking up and taking control of our destiny we reduce our stress. Basically, we stop ourselves from becoming the people we don't rate."

Debra smiled and continued, with Johann, to plan her conversation with her colleague. They worked through what Debra really wanted to achieve and practised separating the facts from the conclusions she was drawing. Debra scripted her opening remarks and then role-played with Johann. They even used video so that Debra was confident in how she came across. Johann reacted in a number of different ways so that, whatever happened, she wouldn't be taken off guard.

Before moving on to plan her discussions with the two bosses, they also agreed when and where Debra was going to approach Yulia so that Debra had a SMART action to take away. The preparation of the second and third conversations went much faster as Debra had begun to internalize the concepts and come to grips with their execution.

When they had finished, Debra sat back. "OK," she said. "You've got me. I can see how – this exercise makes it obvious – being aware of my own emotions and those of others is important in having difficult conversations. But how else can emotional intelligence help in business? This all still seems a bit 'wishy-washy' – it's all very well in academia, but I want to get promoted."

Johann debated internally. Should he tell her how high the stakes were for him too? How he had staked his reputation and the life of the mentoring programme on this very assertion? He decided against it – there may be issues of confidentiality and, in any case, why put more pressure on Debra?

"Let's look back at the definition, before I give you some examples," he suggested. The two definitions, one from Salovey and Mayer and the other, his own, were still on the whiteboard.

> The ability to perceive emotion, integrate emotion to facilitate thought, understand emotions and to regulate emotions to promote personal growth. (Salovey and Mayer)

> It's about being able to notice emotions and understand them so that we can use them when they're useful and manage them when they're not.

"There's going to be some overlap because, obviously, you can't use emotions without understanding and noticing them and noticing emotions is not an effective end in itself. Imagine you were going into a negotiation or, to put it another way, a conflict resolution. And remember, managing conflict is pretty much most of the job after a certain level. You'd want to be aware of any behaviour that suggests emotions on the part of the other side and you'd certainly like to be aware of the impact your own, inevitable and biologically based emotions, are having on your own behaviour.

"For example, some studies show that when we are in a good mood our decision-making changes because we are more optimistic – we think we are healthier than we are, that the economy is improving and that Paris is a better example of a city than Calcutta. Remember, this happens to us all. But if we are very emotionally intelligent, we can be aware of it and can adjust for it or use it. I'd certainly want to be aware if I was being overly optimistic in rating the likelihood of a project succeeding just because I'd slept well, it was sunny and my kids had aced a test!

"It's not about making you more or less clever, in the usual sense. Rather it's about adopting a set of behaviours that allow you to notice, understand, and use or manage emotions." Johann took a breath.

"Can you give me another example of 'understanding emotions?'" Debra asked.

"OK, in that same negotiation you might also use your understanding to decide to use a tool like matching their body language, subtly, to manage emotions – yours and theirs – and to help build rapport that way and so be in a better position to build trust.

"It's about knowing how and why emotions occur, and knowing that this may be different across cultures and other potential 'dividers,' like generation or sex or race.

"For instance, emotionally intelligent individuals know that employees can become anxious when there is a potential threat, such as the possibility of further lay-offs because a recent round has just taken place. So what? Any normally functioning human being can work that out. But they also know that the fact that one of these lay-offs was a one-off and happened in a small company in Tokyo to a 43-year-old man, and the other was part of a restructuring after a merger of two multinationals means that the emotions in all the people involved are different. The messages they need to hear, how they will hear them, and the likely behaviours they will exhibit are different. They may not get the details right because they may not have culturally specific knowledge, but they will at least know what questions to ask."

"The messages they need to hear? You're assuming people will even listen. Most people are just listening for proof that they're right." Debra interjected.

"See how emotionally intelligent you are!" Johann teased. "You're right of course. Many corporate messages are listened to with something on the scale from indifference to contempt. And I think EI can help here too.

"People have been burned in the past by messages that went beyond not noticing potential and entirely predictable emotions to almost actively trying to annoy people. Think of all those people who get fired by SMS or are told that a redundancy is an 'opportunity to start the rest of their career'. It may be true, but it's not exactly sensitive and it's not likely to win friends with the people who now don't have a pay-cheque.

"Would it be so hard to say, as is patently the case, 'This sucks. I'm sorry' and, if you mean it, 'let me know what I can do to help?'. And wouldn't you be more likely to be believed now and in the future if you did behave like that?

"That's why the whole 'authentic' leadership is talked about so much. It's exhausting pretending to be someone you're not and, in any case, it doesn't last. No-one can keep it up indefinitely – especially under stress. Emotional intelligence is fundamental to authentic leadership."

"OK," Debra sensed they might be going off track. "What about using and managing emotions? Can you explain more about that?"

"I might decide to allow a negative emotion to stand, for example if my son is ashamed because he was caught cheating at a school test. I may be happy (another emotion!) to let him feel that because it will help reinforce the behaviour I don't want, that is cheating.

"Or, and this happened just the other day, I might use other information (maybe just past experience) to predict an emotion and then help another person to recognize it and manage it." Before he continued, Johann paused to consider what elements he could share and still retain confidentiality.

"One of my team did a psychometric evaluation the other day which they shared with me," he said.

Debra was amazed. She couldn't imagine sharing something so intimate with her boss or colleagues unless she was forced to.

"This report reinforced other information I had about his emotions. And the most interesting thing, or at least the thing my colleague was most interested in and I remembered, was that this colleague doesn't like conflict and will go to great lengths to avoid it. This rang true to me. I had noticed that he usually stays quiet, preferring not to participate. That's bad enough, but eventually he will blow and there are warning signs just beforehand – he starts to stammer a little and his eyes close slightly. We were in a meeting just a day or two after he shared the evaluation with me and I noticed this happening – the stammering and the eyes. Because we'd discussed it and we had the assessment to refer to rather than just my own thoughts, I felt safe asking for a short break and took the chance to speak with him and tell him what I'd noticed. He had an opportunity to calm down and to raise the issue in a better way."

"That wouldn't always work. I had a colleague who would have taken that as a personal insult," Debra objected.

"You're right, of course. But I bet he wouldn't react the same way if his mother told him. Or his best friend. You need to have built a trusting relationship in advance. Especially because many people assume the worst intentions.

"And, look, even if you can help the other person to manage their emotions it might not be enough – to really get the most out of it the individual you help has to have a high enough EI to then use that information. In this case that didn't happen. The guy did calm down but he went back into silent mode and didn't speak up again. He didn't have the skills. I mean, he was capable of reacting well when I brought the evidence to him, but he wasn't able to own those emotions publicly and manage them. Instead he pushed them down so that they manifested themselves in the stammering and the eyes. It's as though he thought nobody would notice that he was furious. But, of course, we all did.

"None of us brought it up either. And I don't know why – what are we so worried about? Maybe it's because we're afraid of what might happen – if we start talking about emotions maybe people will cry or punch each other? We know we don't have the tools to deal with emotions and so we back away, scared. It reminds me of a recurring dream I had when I was a kid – fighting with my little brother in the back of a car and the car going out of control. I wasn't able to save us. I had that dream for years. Until I learned to drive in fact." He trailed off.

"So you're saying that being the only person with EI gives you an edge but the real edge comes from everyone having it. The total sum is more than the sum of its parts?"

"Yes. And that's why the best leaders use this explicitly. They make it part of business as usual. Because emotions are part of business as usual!" Johann seemed exasperated.

Taking a chance, Debra ventured "You can see why people might prefer to just go on some technical training?"

Johann grimaced. "Yes. You go away and you come back and you've learned something and it can be tested. Absolutely. Much easier. But just because this is harder to measure it doesn't mean it's not valuable. Imagine the possibilities of improving your EI? Did you know that there are studies that show that pleasant emotions can make employees think more creatively, whilst, in contrast, unpleasant emotions can help employees focus on specific problems or issues? Think what I could do to the HR department at salary review time in the name of making them focus!"

Debra laughed. She was 90 per cent sure he was joking. "OK. But let's not get carried away – even if you could do it – it might be more trouble than it's worth? The effect might be small and how do you even know it'll work on the HR people? What is the validity of the study?"

"It's a great question. I've always liked the description of the social sciences as 'where science meets art' so of course you need to exercise some caution. Many of the studies you see reported are actually thinly veiled PR puff pieces and, when you look closer, you realize the sample sizes were tiny or insufficient in some other way. Or maybe there was no control group.

"And, look, even if the study is 100 per cent spot-on, there are so many things that can go wrong that a little knowledge can be a dangerous thing. The key is to focus on a few behaviours that will help you to improve your ability to notice, question and listen. In my experience you'll be amazed at the results of simply showing your interest in others. The key to success in the matrix is relationships or 'friends' and knowing this is important isn't new. Think about Dale Carnegie's famous quote: 'You can make more friends in two months by becoming interested in other people than you can in two years by trying to get other people interested in you'."

"In your opinion, which of the skills is the most difficult?" Debra asked.

"Hmmm. I think I'll have to say noticing because what we notice is so related to who we are. It's hard to imagine other people are noticing something else. I think this is particularly true across cultures.

"I remember walking down a road in Sri Lanka and noticing that there were a lot of different types of green, identifying three species of tree and feeling pleased with myself for spotting a budding Bodhi tree.

"I spoke to my Sri Lankan companion and asked him what he had noticed when walking down the road and at first he didn't understand the question. He didn't think of it as 'noticing' any more than I would think of it as 'noticing' to be aware of the next stop of the train I'm riding. It's just information I need to keep my life going.

"When he did understand my strange question it transpired that he could name 25 different trees and plants alongside many other things I had missed and that the Bodhi tree wasn't a Bodhi tree at all!"

"So even when you remember to look, what you notice might be wrong too?"

"Exactly. Like when Japanese people smile and laugh. Sometimes that means they're happy but it also can mean they're embarrassed. I suppose this means I think understanding is hard too."

"All of the skills are hard," Debra suggested.

"You're right. But it's worth it I think," said Johann. "Think about it, we don't buy from someone we don't trust or like.

So a person who has a high ability to recognize, identify and feel emotions in him/herself and others will be able to build up trust and a good relationship and so sell more easily. And we're all sales people, remember? We all have to sell something, even if it's an idea, to someone else. People with high EI will likely have more friends and mentors in companies and thus advance faster and be able to solicit more backers for their proposals than a person of equal (or perhaps greater) IQ."

"It doesn't mean the proposal or the idea doesn't have to be good. Just that you're more likely to get a hearing if you have high EI."

"Yes. And you are more likely to be able to frame the proposal so that it takes into account all of the concerns and ambitions of your audience."

Johann looked at his watch. They needed to finish up soon if he was to be ready for his next meeting. "What's the alternative?" he asked. "To be owned by our emotions? It is self-evident that emotions impact our behaviour and I believe that leadership is about noticing these emotions and their impact while properly managing that information. We have to be able to do it first for ourselves and then, if we're really good, to help others do the same. All the time acknowledging that we're human and can always slip up and can always get better."

"Do you know what?" Debra interrupted. "This is great news. It means that there is a key to success that I can now learn and so become fabulously successful!" She raised her arms diva-style.

"Hmm," Johann wasn't sure he wanted to get into that discussion right now. "Tell you what, we seem to be out of time. You're all set for your conversations? Then good luck! I'm looking forward to hearing how they go. Give me a call if you need anything and, if not, I'll see you next week."

They both stood up as Debra collected her notes and left.

 Key Takeaways

1. *People with high EI will likely have more friends and mentors in companies and thus advance faster and be able to solicit more backers for their proposals than a person of equal (or perhaps a greater) IQ.*

2. *If you can learn the mental skills that come along with EI, you will be able to get better at the behaviours that underpin success in the matrix.*

3. *Not speaking up means that nothing changes, meaning you miss a great opportunity to help yourself and your colleagues at the same time.*

4. *Being aware of your own emotions and those of others is important in having difficult conversations as well as in other key workplace situations.*

11

Why IQ isn't Enough

"OK you've convinced me." Debra got straight down to business as she brought coffee for the two of them. "I think the definition you have of EI is useful and I can see how EI helps in managing or mastering the matrix. But can it help us recruit better people? How can we test EI? And how is EI different from EQ which I see referred to in some of the articles you sent me?"

"I think EI and EQ refer to the same thing," Johann replied. "EI is emotional intelligence and EQ is emotional quotient which I think is meant to remind us of IQ or what I suppose we must call 'general intelligence'. I prefer EI because I think it focuses the mind on the fact that it's about having intelligence around emotions and the ability to improve that. I don't like EQ because the focus seems to be on the emotions which doesn't seem very helpful as surely everybody has an EQ or, to put it another way, an amount of emotions that they will experience and react to. Emotional intelligence – EI – is about having the ability to acknowledge these emotions so that you can use them or manage them effectively."

"I'm still not sure why there has to be an emotional 'intelligence'. Isn't IQ enough?" Debra's cynicism seemed to have returned.

"Look, according to studies in the 1980s and 1990s, there was less than a 25 per cent correlation between IQ, or general intelligence, and success (measured as academic achievement and occupational status) so there is a lot left to account for. We've all heard stories of taxi drivers with PhDs. Or met crazy bright guys working behind bars or in 35 degree heat as labourers. Or the woman who never learned to read so who knows how bright she is? Obviously many factors come into play – dumb luck of birth included – but let's say that EI is even just part of the other 75 per cent? I'd say it's worth looking at."

Debra agreed. "OK. But it's extraordinarily difficult to get people to own emotions. I remember seeing an external facilitator who asked a group how they were feeling and he had to ask five different times before they would use an adjective. They said things like 'he shouted' or, when pressed, would admit something about the other person's emotions, for example, 'he's obviously angry' but then wouldn't admit they had an emotion about that.

"And I've noticed that people often avoid acknowledging emotions, or signs of emotion, if they feel that they've won. I saw a guy the other day who finished the meeting with a hearty 'So glad we've all agreed!' when, actually, at least 40 per cent of the people in the room weren't convinced. The ones who seemed convinced were split into those who didn't understand it and those who didn't care. This must have been obvious to him. Or it should have been. But he seemed genuinely surprised when the plan didn't get put into action and everybody started to avoid him."

"Couldn't he have scared them into submission, into doing what they promised?"

Johann was joking but Debra took him seriously. "OK. Fine but fear is an emotion. If the person doing the scaring is doing it intentionally – a teacher or a parent with kids for example or a boss laying out a serious situation – and they're aware of the impact they're having and have considered then that's fine. Those people have emotional intelligence – you might question their conclusions but their methods are sound and they may know something you don't.

"But if they are doing it by default – without making any judgements or even being aware that there are decisions to make and other options available – that's a different story. Same thing if they don't know the impact they are having or don't care. And if they don't have any other options then they certainly aren't high in EI. That's what I think!"

Debra seemed quite exercised by the thought and stopped for a moment. Then, as if to back up her opinion, she continued. "Warren Buffett is probably high in EI – I think I remember he wrote something about using love over fear in leading others."

"Really?" Johann made a note to look it up later.

"So, how can we make sure we hire people with high EI? Can we test for it?" Debra returned to her original question.

"Some of the experts in this field seem to believe, more or less, that there's no point in many of the assessments out there because they are self-reported and let's face it, we can all think of someone who believes themselves to be emotionally intelligent but has genuinely no idea how he comes across to others. Or knows how they come across but believes that they don't have a choice or that the other person (more likely, people) needs to change for them. There are people who continue to believe that the problem is how they are perceived and not how they act, even when that belief makes their lives harder. And they know it."

Debra could think of a number of individuals like this.

Johann continued: "But even the ability-based tests, like the one Mayer and some of his colleagues developed, are a bit problematical because although they ask people how they *would* behave, people tend to answer based on what they know or feel about how they *should* behave. Those are two very different things! And even if it works there's the problem that you're only measuring ability rather than the individual's potential to learn or get more able at this 'soft stuff,' which is surely important?"

Debra looked at Johann and asked: "So is there a test you like?"

Johann thought. "You can measure your EI using Mayer and Salovey's model with the," he took a deep breath, "Mayer–Salovey–Caruso Emotional Intelligence Test (MSCEIT). It tests your abilities on each of Mayer and Salovey's four branches of emotional intelligence by asking you a number of questions and generating scores for each of the branches as well as a total score."

"Just like an IQ test," Debra suggested.

"Yes. But central to the four-branch model is the idea that EI requires attunement to social norms so the," he took another deep breath, "MSCEIT is not scored like an IQ test. It's scored in a consensus fashion, with higher scores indicating higher overlap between an individual's answers and those provided by a worldwide sample of respondents. The MSCEIT can also be expert-scored, so that the amount of overlap is calculated between an individual's answers and those provided by a group of 21 emotion researchers."

"So there's no right or wrong answers? That's weird!"

"Quite," Johann agreed. "And the consensus scoring criterion means that it is impossible to create questions that only a minority of respondents can solve, because, by definition, responses are deemed emotionally 'intelligent' only if the majority of the sample has endorsed them."

"So there's only one answer (not right or wrong but 'agreed' on) and also no way of telling who is better than who? That doesn't seem to make much sense?"

"I can't say I disagree. But, ultimately I'm not sure it's as important as just figuring out that EI is important and trying to get better at it. I'll wait until someone cleverer than me works out a valid test and trust my gut until then. In any case, let's hope I'm right and let's not worry too much because our work is about preparing you for success in the matrix and, in the matrix, where you are trying to get people over whom you have no direct control or authority to do things, it may be the most important tool you've got. You need to be able to influence others and you can't do that without being able to notice emotions and understand them so that you can use them when they're useful and manage them when they're not. Which is of course our definition of EI."

"Well, it does matter because if you can't test for it how can you learn it?"

"Interesting that you say learn and not teach," Johann mused. "Anyway, I just don't see the connection you're making as valid; I disagree that you can't learn stuff that can't be tested for – we do all the time – it's just harder to prove anything has changed. We need to be smarter at testing. For example, how will we test if this mentoring has been any use?" As he finished the question Johann realized that he was potentially on dangerous ground.

"I suppose it's about how I feel at the end," Debra suggested.

"Absolutely. Anything else?"

"And about how others feel about me? Including you?" Debra wasn't sure.

"How they feel about you?"

"Yes. Whether they feel that they have more trust in me, that I understand them better and communicate better – that kind of thing. Because emotions are real even if they're not."

It was Johann's turn to look confused.

"I mean that emotions are real to people even if they're not based in fact. They can be based on a misinterpretation – if

I feel like someone has snubbed me, then I will behave as though they've snubbed me, whether it's true or not. They'll then react to that behaviour and so it goes on. It's about the perception and, in the same way, my progress is advanced or hindered by how I'm perceived by others."

"Ah, I see," Johann agreed. "Yes. EI should give you the ability to notice that you are making assumptions and having emotions and so you should be able to stop the spiral. Or to ask for help before it starts. For example, I'm obsessed with punctuality and get very angry when people are late but I'm in a culture where that isn't seen the same way. With my team, we've agreed that there will be an eight- minute grace period for arriving at the start of a meeting and if I show signs of getting impatient before that someone reminds me that I'm not in New York anymore!

"To answer your question: I'm convinced we can learn EI. Remember it's not about personality traits or characteristics. Think about it like learning to drive a car or ride a horse – everyone can do it but some people will find it easier than others or be better at learning. And what makes it easier or harder, beyond raw talent, is stuff like the kind of teacher, the amount of practise, your motivations, the environment you grew up in – there's not that many people growing up surrounded by horses who don't become good riders. There are many different things that can affect how we learn EI."

Debra broke in, "So you're saying it's like with any other skill we all start from different places when it comes to our natural ability to carry out the various behaviours. A dancer might be very good at doing plies but not be great at the splits for example.

"And we can't change the raw talent we're born with but if this stuff is important – and we've agreed it is – then it's worthwhile spending time learning. If you can learn the mental skills that come along with EI you will be able to get better at the behaviours that underpin success in the matrix. Because they will help you build relationships and these are the foundation of how work gets done.

"And you can succeed without EI but, without those skills, people get frustrated and stressed and morale and perform-ance suffer because people spend time playing games and not speaking up."

"Exactly. And it can be dangerous too. Imagine if some of those bankers had spoken up before the financial crisis? When they saw the way things were going? How much grief might we have been spared!" Johann realized that he was in danger of setting off on a particular hobby-horse. "Oops I'm off again. That's enough about EI for now. Tell me, how did it go with the bosses and Yulia?"

"Actually, it was a mixed bag," Debra admitted. "The conversation with Yulia was great. As it turned out she had no idea how much her behaviour was affecting me and she's identified some actions that she's going to take that will make life easier. But one of my bosses reacted very badly – he practically accused me of trying to 'divide and conquer' by driving a wedge between him and the other guy."

"Ouch," Johann interjected. "So what did you do?"

"Well, it wasn't too bad as, if you remember, we'd identified this as one possible way the conversation might go – that my boss might be suspicious. I was able to notice it and react to it by apologizing for the misunderstanding. I attempted to make clear that, in fact, I was trying to get their help in managing the conflicting demands on my time."

They continued to debrief the conversations Debra had had during the week and finished up some time later. It wasn't until she was back at her desk, with this week's "homework" that Debra realized she hadn't got to the bottom of how you would go about learning to improve your emotional intelligence.

Key Takeaways

1. *EI stands for emotional intelligence and EQ is emotional quotient. They refer to the same thing but with a slightly different focus in each case.*

2. *According to studies in the 1980s and 1990s, there was less than a 25 per cent correlation between IQ, or general intelligence, and success so there is a lot left to account for.*

3. *Many tests of EI are of dubious value because they rely on self-reporting or prediction. No test offers to identify individuals who have high EI potential.*

4. *You need to be able to influence others and you can't do that without being able to notice emotions and understand them so that you can use them when they're useful and manage them when they're not.*

12

Learning EI

D ebra continued to think about how she should learn EI. She asked an internal training expert for advice on what her options were. The trainer, Judith, suggested she enrol in a two-day public course on emotional intelligence, or she could wait and join an internal programme running in four months. She decided to talk to some of her colleagues who had attended the internal session in the past and, whilst all of them said it was interesting, few of them seemed to think that they were acting much differently as a result.

After this research, Debra's scepticism seemed well founded. It appeared that the traditional training courses either didn't share any of the background research, so the attendees weren't convinced of the importance of EI. Because of this oversight her colleagues didn't engage. Or the trainers explained the background in a very academic way so the importance of these behaviours was lost. People realized they weren't going to learn practical skills, so they returned to their phones and laptops.

Not to mention the content and delivery seemed a bit "fuzzy" to Debra's colleagues – not quite middle-aged ladies talking about "The Secret" but close enough to allow many to dismiss the subject outright. Elena, her colleague in HR, had even said: "I couldn't take it seriously. It was like they had discovered the holy grail. Which meant it couldn't be questioned. And if you did question them, they couldn't tell you what it was made of!"

All of the courses devoted a significant amount of time to practising behaviours which everyone seemed to think useful. But when people returned to their offices with a set of new skills that were thereafter ignored, sooner or later, the ability and even the knowledge behind those skills atrophied. Debra wanted something meatier. Something that would "stick".

So you can definitely learn it, she thought. She had read some work by Daniel Goleman, the author Johann had mentioned who wrote about EI. He talked about a set of emotional competencies which are not innate talents, but rather learned capabilities. These capabilities must be worked on and can be developed to achieve outstanding performance. The problem is: no-one seemed very clear on how.

Debra thought about learning to drive: *I certainly started at a low level there and didn't have much, or any, natural talent. The classes helped, of course. I mean, I learned the basics – the concepts and the theory – and I had a chance to practise the behaviours. But it took me ages to get good at it. Maybe it's like that with EI?*

She was pretty sure she could pass a test like the one developed by Mayer and his colleagues. And, under ideal or classroom conditions, she was sure she could display the behaviours needed. Debra wasn't convinced, however, that it would really make a difference when under emotional stress. Would what she learned come back when she needed it most?

Debra remembered reading once that the best way to learn something was to do so in circumstances that most resemble those in which you will use the knowledge or skill. *If that's true*, she thought, *then I need a chance to practise and debrief on real-life situations.*

Debra remembered vaguely a "ladder of learning" or "ladder of competence" that a trainer had shown her years ago. Googling it, she found an image that clarified her thinking immediately.

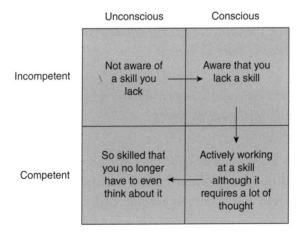

	Unconscious	Conscious
Incompetent	Not aware of a skill you lack	Aware that you lack a skill
Competent	So skilled that you no longer have to even think about it	Actively working at a skill although it requires a lot of thought

So training can tell us what to do and give us some chance to practise, but the real key is trying new behaviours in real life or as close to real life as possible. That's exactly what I'm worried about, she thought: *moving from stage 3 to stage 4. I don't see how even the best trainer can do that for me. And without that progress I think it'd be very easy to slip back to stage 2 again. And that's the worst of all worlds – knowing you're not good at something but not getting better. How depressing!*

What I really need is someone to act as a cheerleader or as a sponsor like recovering addicts might have. That makes sense, she thought, *recovering addicts are certainly trying to change their behaviour!*

I need someone who will remind me what I'm supposed to do, who will keep me on the straight and narrow, give me confidence when I need it and a kicking when that's what will work. Interesting, she thought. *It's like the advice they give you when you go on a diet or start an exercise regime – get a buddy!*

But I don't just want a buddy, she thought. *I want someone to teach me – who could do that?*

Not my manager, that's for sure, she thought. She almost laughed out loud. When Johann had talked about people who would self-report as having EI but actually were as emotionally intelligent as a dead toad she had immediately pictured her current manager! Could a different manager do it? Yes. But they'd have to be very self-aware. And motivated enough to take the time necessary away from their day job.

How would such a manager behave? What would he or she have to do to help you get better at EI? Debra couldn't imagine where you would start to help someone get better at noticing, using and managing their own emotions. And then notice those of the people around them as well. She made a mental note to discuss this with Johann and went back to an issue that had been bothering her recently, although she was starting to see the situation differently as a result of her work with him.

Since learning about the matrix it had occurred to her that one of its advantages ought to be that it's easier to avoid group think because people move around, so norms don't get accepted over time. However, in one of the projects Debra was working on, there was a very strong project manager, Andy. He had lots of great points but he was very, Debra thought about the right word, forceful. The project had been going on for a long time – longer than anticipated – so most of the other people on the project team knew him well and they had learned to avoid giving him bad news because his violent reactions (mostly shouting and sarcasm) made it too dangerous. It was one of the reasons the project was so far behind!

A new IT guy had just joined the team and he challenged one of Andy's assumptions. He was very reasonable, not cheeky or disrespectful in any way. But Andy blew up. He turned on the guy and destroyed him. He didn't raise his voice but his tone and words were cutting and belittling so that he seemed almost threatening. Debra had watched this new guy deflate as he physically cringed under the assault. He hadn't spoken once at the next meeting. Debra hadn't known what to do at the time so, along with everyone else, she did nothing. She was determined to discuss this with Johann so that they could think about what might be going on and come up with ideas about what steps to take in order to fix the problem.

She also wanted to let him know that in the last few days she realized, simply by thinking about it and remembering to notice, that she worked best when she was under a certain amount of pressure. She further noticed that for her the "best" pressure came from having promised something to a peer. So, to avoid procrastination and being overwhelmed at the last minute, she had now set up a system whereby she had to deliver "first-stage deliverables" and "second-stage deliverables" to peers with whom she worked. So far it seemed to be helping.

Wow, she thought. *Johann has really done a number on me. I've gone from not thinking about emotions to thinking about them, noticing them and using them too. I wonder where that puts me on that "ladder of learning?"*

 Key Takeaways

1. *Learning EI and moving up the "ladder of learning" from unconscious incompetence to conscious competence takes time and deliberate practise.*

2. *Undergoing a training course or test may prove useful in some respects but what you learn may not come back when under real emotional stress.*

3. *The best way to learn something is to do so in circumstances that most resemble those in which you will use the knowledge or skill.*

4. *The real key is finding the opportunities to practise and debrief on real-life situations.*

5. *Having a "cheerleader," coach or sponsor help you to get better at noticing, using and managing your emotions can prove effective.*

13

Fake It Until You Make It

Debra was excited: "You've been using EI on me all along and teaching me to use it even whilst I was learning about it." It was almost an accusation.

"That's true." Johann responded mildly. He had been expecting this. In fact, he was surprised it had taken so long.

"Why didn't you tell me?"

"What would have been the point?" he asked gently. "You didn't believe in EI or see any use for it in business in general and the matrix in particular. So instead of telling you what I was doing I just did it and waited for you to figure it out yourself. But, remember, I did say that I'd be transparent and I will. It just wasn't the right time before now."

Debra smiled. "So go on . . . ," she challenged.

"What, you want me to reveal my secrets?" Johann pretended to be shocked. "Actually I do have a list."

"Of secrets?" Debra's sarcasm was apparent.

"Well, yes. I mean, they're not secrets but I think they are the 'secret to EI'. I'm working on the 'fake it until you make it' principle here but it seems to work or at least it did for me. Years back I had a mentor – I didn't call him that of course – and he was always able to get great results from the people around him even when they didn't work for him. People opened up to him and trusted him. Everybody liked this guy so, over the years, I started to note down the things he did, and mimicked them. I didn't really understand why. Then, I added to the list when I saw other people do things that seemed to help them. When I started looking into EI I realized that my list was pretty much a set of tools to help you 'fake' EI or, to put it another way, to practise in a way that helps you get better at it.

"It's a very practical list. Basically what I tried to do was break down what people did – their practice or skill if you like – into the smallest possible units of behaviour. I've called them the tools. Then all I had to do was use those tools a lot. Over time I got better at using most of them and in some of them I'm really good now. I still struggle with others."

So he's on different rungs of the ladder with the different tools, Debra thought. "What do you mean you broke the skills into tools?" she asked.

"Well, let's take presenting as an example. Presenting is a skill and my test for this is: 'if someone tells you to get better at this, can you do it without more information?'. Like, someone says, 'Debra, you need to work on your presentation skills'. How useful is that?"

"Not very."

"Exactly. So we don't teach presentation skills or EI. Not if we want to do it properly. We break down what makes a good presenter – what do they do? And what does someone with high EI do? Because we can do something useful with that. We can teach that. And those tools are multi-purpose – they can be used to help you do lots of different things."

"I see," Debra said. "Can you give me an example?" If not quite on the edge of her seat, Debra was certainly interested.

"Take misaligned goals as an example. How much time and energy do you think is wasted in the average organization because of misaligned goals?"

Debra assumed this was a rhetorical question.

"If you read up about EI you'll be told that having high EI helps with dealing with misaligned goals. You'll learn that emotionally intelligent individuals manage their emotions well when goals are discussed. They know it's normal to feel frustration and stress when goals are misaligned, and they have the ability to manage their frustration and stress and prevent these emotions from rising to the point that their discussions become unproductive. They can predict the stress the misaligned goals will cause to themselves and others and so raise their concerns in advance. And they can communicate their concerns so that people respond favourably. This is all very well. But it doesn't tell you what to do!

"Training will tell you what to do of course. If you do training in EI you'll learn that it's important to, for example, listen or find mutual cause. But the only way you'll actually get better at doing those things, to dealing with misaligned goals is if you actually use these tools." Johann seemed surprised at the audacity of his own claims.

"So you're saying that the things on this list are like a magic bullet?"

"No. I'm saying that they're all highly gifted bullets. None of them alone can do everything although each one in itself is powerful; but together they're much more powerful than when used separately."

"Can't wait to hear them," Debra deadpanned.

Johann leaned back and, counting with his fingers counted off:

1. Use your senses
2. Consider emotions
3. Reflect what you notice
4. Acknowledge what you hear
5. Incorporate what you learn
6. Reiterate what you hear
7. Check for confirmation
8. Change when there's a better idea
9. Know why you do things, ask others
10. Review regularly
11. Ask "so what?"
12. Look out for obstacles
13. Calibrate
14. Focus on both the other person and yourself

"Seems like some of these at least can be understood in more than one way?" Debra enquired.

"Absolutely, but that's OK. It doesn't have to be detailed. Think of it as an aide memoire, something you can refer back to when explaining things to other people. And this way you see the tools as being multipurpose. You only have 14 things to remember to get better at. And you can tell if you're doing them or not.

"Only 14?"

"No, you're right. There's 15! Last but not least there is the one that is both the easiest and the hardest:

15. Do what you say you will do

"I'm surprised that listening isn't on the list?" Debra asked.

Johann was agitated. "But it is on the list. What do you think listening is? 'Reflect what you notice,' 'Acknowledge what you hear,' 'Check for confirmation' and so on – I would argue if you can do all of the things I just said on the list, you'd be a pretty good listener!

"The idea is to break things down so that you or somebody else can SEE or HEAR you do the behaviour/use the tool. That way it's a mechanical thing. Almost anyone can remember to check for confirmation – it's not hard. But few people know how to get better at listening. This set of tools is supposed to be really practical.

"It's like professional golfers. They might be working on 100 things with their coach, but they won't try to change all of these during the act of playing an important round. They'll step on the tee of a competition focusing on doing one thing better. Play 18 holes, take stock, monitor improvement. They go off and work on all aspects again with the coach, then back to the course for another competitive round – with just one 'swing thought' in their heads. They might use the same thought again the next round, or they might move on to another aspect. They're always working on changes, but in bite-sized pieces to affect measurable change.

"We need to break things down into bite-sized pieces that we can work on."

"But some of these will depend on others. Like if one tool isn't working properly then the others will not work at full capacity either."

"True enough," Johann admitted. "But, and this is the rub, you can probably only work on one or maybe two things at a time if you're going to do it properly. Three at a real push. And even if it's only one then at least you're getting better at one thing. When you've done that you can start on the next. I mean, what are your other options? Give up?"

"OK. Can you give me some examples of these tools at work?"

"Sure. Research has found that decisions in matrix organizations are more untimely and can be of lower quality than in traditional forms of organization, although, of course, better decision making should be part of the advantages of the matrix. Emotionally intelligent individuals recognize that some emotions are likely and look out for them. When they think they spot them they confirm the emotion and its source and, the emotion out there and acknowledged, they then choose how to behave from the various options open to them. For example, they might work to defuse any anger because they know that the research suggests it leads people to make snap judgements – they do not consider the available information and the possible consequences. Or they might increase anxiety to influence more thorough processing of information or induce happiness for more creativity.

"Can you make the connection? Between what I've just described and the tools on the list?"

Debra looked at the notes she had scribbled as Johann listed the 15 tools.

1. Use your senses
2. Consider emotions
3. Reflect what you notice
4. Acknowledge what you hear
5. Incorporate what you learn
6. Reiterate what you hear
7. Check for confirmation
8. Change when there's a better idea
9. Know why you do things, ask others
10. Review regularly
11. Ask "so what?"
12. Look out for obstacles
13. Calibrate
14. Focus on both the other person and yourself
15. Do what you say you will do

"Yes, they would have to use all of them. Even 15. 'Do what you say you will do' but that is pretty much the case in every situation."

"How do you make out that they'd have to review regularly?"

"Well, they must review the business literature regularly to know about the research you described."

"Good point! I'll have to add that interpretation to the master list."

Debra was intrigued to see this master list but did not, yet, ask Johann for it. "I still don't see how you teach this though? I mean, beyond a certain level."

"That's true. But it's probably true of most skills. I mean, once you've learned the basics of riding a bike, how do you teach somebody to get better?"

"I suppose it depends. Once you get past the basics. Yes, and so training in EI focuses on the basics, and, if you're lucky, you'll get a chance to use some of the tools although probably not in a way that makes it clear that you can use each of them in lots of different ways. But to get really good, what do you need to do? How can you teach somebody to get really good at EI?"

"Well, I'm not sure," Johann admitted. "But I think it's mostly about being an example (like the guy I learned from), then, after that, you can be transparent about the tools you're using and after that it'll probably depend on the individual. The 'teacher' needs to have high EI and try different things, notice what happens and then make adjustments. After the basics you don't really teach; you help the other person to learn. But I suppose there are a few tools to add to the list that could be especially useful to 'teachers'."

"Like what?" Debra asked.

"I'm still learning about this so the list is changing more. Let me find it." Johann opened his desk drawer. "I've added:

1. Have some stock questions."
    He explained. "Like 'say more about X' or 'anything else?' because you're human and your concentration will slip at times and you won't know what they were talking about. And because sometimes simple questions are the best. The three questions to deal with the three 'clever stories' of victims, villains and helplessness are a great example of a stock question that you can use a lot.
2. Go at their pace – you will do anyway! There's no point in expecting people to do things they aren't capable of. No matter how much you motivate them

it won't make a difference if they don't have the skills. You have to gauge things very carefully.

3. Share – your own experiences and emotions but remember it's about them.

4. Ask good questions – to yourself and others. At the right time, in the right place, for the right reasons. I have pontificated a bit in our sessions but I've asked some questions too I hope?"

Debra nodded.

"I didn't have to ask too many questions or try too hard with you as you opened up. But you can always get better at asking questions – both to yourself and others. They're useful in so many ways that this tool should probably be some kind of mega tool. A power tool! So we now have 15 tools and a power tool! One that you can use in many ways – to get clarity, to confirm, to probe, to doubt, to get details so you can build understanding and then empathy.

"But the most important thing another person can do is help you to practise – to work through in slow time – like we did, in advance. We're creatures of habit and practising helps us build good ones. And helps us feel confident enough to try things in real life.

"But, look, no teacher is going to be perfect. That 'ladder of learning' we talked about has more than four rungs. The fifth rung is reflective ability, or 'conscious competence of uncon-scious incompetence' and that leads you to noticing where you can still improve so you slip back to the third rung for a time. Which is good because that's how you stay sharp."

You're sharp but not the tool? Debra thought. "How do you use the detailed list?" she said aloud.

"Well, now I know it by heart of course. Although I still read it before big deal meetings and look at it once a week. And I ask myself what I should add or take away. I don't want to let it get too big as it stops being useful I think. Once a quarter I choose one of the tools and ask someone to observe me just using that and to give me feedback. I force myself to become more aware of that tool and my use of it and I sometimes tell people what I'm working on and ask for their help.

"The thing is – it's not complicated but it does take commitment.

"What you're trying to do is help someone to move up the rungs from unconscious incompetence to conscious compe-tence. You start where they are and you help them but it's their responsibility to do the work.

"As they get better you point out what they're doing well and give them a heads up on what is stopping them from getting to the next level. Like when a kid learns to walk – eventually they get really good at it and run and then they get good at that. But to be a professional runner you need to deconstruct your run before you can reconstruct it. A coach can help but the work is up to the runner. It's up to them to practise and the coach or mentor or whoever can help by asking them to reflect and by questioning their thinking and their actions in a useful way.

"Another way I can help is through what Goleman, Boyatzis and McKee call 'a journey of self-discovery and personal reinvention'. They suggest asking a number of questions. Some might find the questions a bit, um 'American?' if you know what I mean?"

Debra nodded. "What are they?" Johann found the slide and flashed it on the screen.

Who do I want to be?
Who am I now?
How do I get from here to there?
How do I make change stick?
Who can help me?

"I know," he said, anticipating Debra's response. "But imagine if you were able to stop yourself in the middle of a flash of anger and answer those questions before you reacted. Just like in the *Crucial Conversations* book. That would be useful, right?"

Debra agreed. "Obviously."

"Well, the only way to do that is to get to Level 4 on the use of those tools – to be aware that that is what you should be doing and noticing when you do and don't do it, and noting the results and then doing it more and more and better and better until you do it without noticing!"

"Or I achieve Nirvana! It does seem like a lot of work?" Debra suggested.

"Well, yes." Johann didn't seem to have any problem with that. "You don't think your way into a different way of acting; you act your way into a different way of thinking. So many people I talk to want there to be a different answer. There isn't. It's like that training course you mentioned that you went on and liked – The Leadership Challenge? You have to do things differently and that involves pain and heartache sometimes and embarrassment and boredom at other times. But it's worth it because, eventually, it's less exhausting as you're being truly authentic.

"You have no choice but to be authentic because you need to be trusted. You are not only allowed to have a point of view and to state it, you're almost obliged to because you have the tools to do it in a way that will help the situation you find yourself in. So you know your stances on major work issues and are open and willing to engage in conversations about them. This is important because if others are to trust you they need and want to know where you stand – they don't want to have to guess or be blindsided midstream.

"And you can be transparent. EI helps you to understand the difference between navigating the political waters of your organization and actually becoming the politics itself – how to get support for your initiatives but be clear about what you are doing, why you are doing it, and how you are doing it. With high EI you can communicate this to people in a way that they can understand and hear you."

"That does sound worth it." Debra was amused that Johann was still selling the concept to her.

"Of course it is." Johann was in evangelical mode. "These tools are the only game in town."

Debra now felt that there should be more to it. Just using 15 tools and thinking and reflecting on how it went so you get better? And then practising again? Well, she reflected, I suppose it worked for sports stars and musicians and dancers. All I'm really doing is practising a behaviour – just like them, she thought.

Once again Johann seemed to show an uncanny ability to read her mind. "It's like Andy Murray or someone like that." He stopped to check that she got the reference. "He's clearly got an in-born talent."

"True. But it doesn't have to be someone with that job description. If you want to give yourself every chance to succeed in changing your behaviour – something that is notoriously difficult to do – just ask any smoker or coffee drinker. Weirdly, they also say that it's just as important to keep seeing that person when things are going well as during times of stress. Soaring cortisol levels and an added hard kick of adrenaline can paralyse the mind's critical abilities, so people fall back into old habits during these times.

"According to Goleman, leaders can improve their emotional intelligence if they are given:

- Information – candid assessment of their strengths and limitations from people they can trust.
- Guidance – a specific development plan using 'naturally occurring' workplace encounters as the laboratory for learning.
- Support – someone to talk to as they practise how to handle different situations."

"That makes sense to me – you could be describing the job of a great manager or coach or mentor."

"And, because the research suggests that people will vary on how proficient they are at different parts of EI, a generic training course probably won't be much use. For example, some people could be worse at identifying how others feel while others are less adept at managing emotions. So you need one-to-one help to make sure you get the right intervention at the right time and you will certainly need different people at different parts of your career."

"The way you say it seems to take away from what you do – are you really saying anyone could help me?" Debra asked.

"Well, yes and no. I mean it doesn't have to be someone older and wiser and more senior. But it does have to be someone who practices what they preach. These tools aren't hard to use but it takes time to develop the right skill set and, as we discussed before, many people don't take the necessary time.

"There's a story of an external executive coach who was asked by a CEO to work with the CFO. 'Please help me,' the CEO said. 'I can't get this guy to do anything I want!'. 'What do you want him to do?' asked the coach, writing down the answer the CEO gave. The coach then met the CFO and asked him what issue he would like to address. 'My biggest problem,' the CFO said, 'is that I just don't know what this guy wants from me'. The coach asked him if it would be helpful to have a list and, when the CFO agrees, shares it with the CEO. Six weeks later all is peace and productivity with the CFO, so the CEO asks the coach to come in for a meeting. 'You're a genius,' said the CEO. 'How did you do it?'. When the coach explained, the CEO got angry. He felt he'd been tricked. 'Anybody could have done that,' he said. The coach was forced to explain, gently, that that was true. But nobody had."

Debra laughed. "Maybe if the coach had had higher EI he might have anticipated that reaction!"

"Good point," Johann laughed too.

"So yes, it could be anybody who uses the tools, but like an actor who wants to teach other actors, he'd better be able to explain the process. The coach or mentor needs to have that 'Rung 5' level of self-awareness.

"But don't forget, it's about the coachee or mentee or student or whatever you want to call them too – they have to listen and take responsibility for change!

"One thing I forgot to say about how having a mentor or coach is that they should focus you on that responsibility. Their objective is to help you to act in whatever way you've decided will help you. They'll need to understand how to manage your emotions, so that you can eventually do that as well. Your job is to do the work, to try the behaviours. They can help by getting you to focus on potential obstacles and asking great questions. They can make sure you have SMART actions, but as Goleman et al. say: 'the only way to develop your social circuitry effectively is to undertake the hard work of changing your behaviour'."

"OK. I'm convinced. And delighted I have a mentor."

Johann bowed.

"But it must cost a fortune? I mean the basic training alone is expensive and then the coach or mentor. You're not cheap, I assume?"

"Oh yes, it all adds up," Johann admitted. "And we don't even track the expense of people not being at their day jobs because they are attending training or coaching. And for the mentoring or coaching we often don't have enough internal people who are willing and able so we use external suppliers. So yes, it costs. But we need it.

"We need employees who are able to deal with the challenges of the matrix; who can better align various goals, clarify roles and responsibilities, make timely and quality decisions. We need to see results across silos through communication and cooperation. We need people who can build strong bonds because we need those for practical as well as emotional reasons. Those aren't things you learn in one day or even a five-day training session. It takes more time, patience and practice than that.

"Let's imagine a typical matrix situation. There is tension between the function and the geography about a decision

– let's say it's a marketing campaign. The ambiguity inherent in the matrix leads to tension and anxiety among employees as they try to reconcile unclear roles and responsibilities. Now, a key tenet of the matrix design is that tension is inherent and desirable. But research shows that employees who are unaccustomed to the tension and don't have the tools to deal with it spend immense time and energy unsuccessfully trying to reduce it. Often senior management don't notice, or they don't care, suggesting foolishly that 'the tension is built in, live with it'.

"Emotionally intelligent employees are more likely to perceive the tension and its effects, understand the specific issues that are causing the tension, and then facilitate solutions. Those with very high EI are, I bet, able to educate others and help them understand where the tension comes from and strategies for dealing with it.

"Notice that none of the tools are exclusively for use with peers or direct reports. These tools and EI work when you are 'managing up' as well. You need to manage up and across not just when you have a difficult boss, an incompetent colleague or an important project. You need to manage up and across, for example, to get the production guys to see that *your* project will help them meet *their* goals; to establish authority so you are trusted with new projects; to get volunteers. Managing up is about understanding your boss's priorities, pressures and work style. And you can't do that without EI.

"There are times when individuals, especially those who want to advance very quickly, may become manipulative and try to game the matrix. Because they have different reporting lines, they can play people off in the organization and nobody holds them accountable because it's not clear whose job is whose. You might see someone who appears to be cooperative, but in the background they are motivated to achieve something different which will get them rewarded. You need EI to be able to be vocal, to communicate openly with people in a way that makes it likely they will listen.

"EI can be used in the strangest settings. It seems some bill collectors were trained to express calmness when talking to angry debtors and anger when talking to friendly or sad debtors so as to increase the likelihood that they received payments. Obviously this involved all the different aspects of EI. I wonder how they were trained?"

"They would certainly have been motivated!" Debra pointed out.

"Yes, sales people often seem interested in this. I suppose for the same reason – they see an immediate connection and link to their back pocket, but the rest of us have to look a little harder to see the need to build better relationships. We think that doing our job should be enough. Apparently women are particularly bad at this." Johann was aware, as a mentor, of the danger of not acknowledging experiences different from his and so had looked into this area. "As I understand it women are likely to not speak up, hiding their light under a bushel. I suppose we've already talked about you in this respect?"

Debra agreed. "And yet we think of women as having higher EI than men usually."

"Hmmm, interesting point. Maybe women, in general, tend to be better at some things, for example noticing emotions. But this doesn't mean they're good at all parts of EI.

"Anyway, remember the cost of having someone with low EI – the damage they can do to themselves, others and the business in terms of time wasted and absent conversations. It seems to me that we don't have a choice. Either we put the work in and improve our EI, or we accept the frustrations that come with trying to work in a matrix without those tools. Complaining about it will only eventually irritate your co-workers, friends and family. And it won't change a thing."

Debra nodded her agreement as Johann continued.

"But yes, you're right. It's expensive and takes times and effort to do this right and, if you're using internal people – even senior managers like me – you have to make sure those mentors are properly trained. There is no reason to think that they have the necessary skills."

"One last thought – it's OK to have training and a mentor/coach, but what about your manager and their manager?"

"Great question. Now you know how this works you won't be surprised that I'm going to suggest that you consider the answer to this for the next session. What have you seen that worked in the past? What would work for you?"

With that, Johann brought the session to an end and Debra gathered her belongings and left the room.

 Key Takeaways

1. *If you want to get better at something, you need to break it down into bite-sized pieces that you can work on.*

2. *These bite-sized pieces are the behaviours that other people can see or hear. If you can get better at doing these behaviours (using these tools) you can improve your skill.*

3. *We are creatures of habit and practising helps us to build good ones, helping us to feel more confident to try things in real life.*

4. *Practice and reflection is key to improving your EI as "the only way to develop your social circuitry effectively is to undertake the hard work of changing your behaviour."*

5. *If others are to trust you, they need and want to know where you stand – they don't want to have to guess or be blindsided midstream.*

6. *Be aware of, and practise, practise, practise the 15 tools. And share them!*

14

How Managers Can Help Improve EI

Debra spent the next few days observing the managers she worked with and thinking about what they could do to help their colleagues improve their emotional intelligence. She noticed that managers were in a great position to do this. Unlike coaches or mentors, they usually saw the behaviours, or lack of them, in real time. They could assess and react immediately, with specific feedback and supportive coaching. Of course, this feedback only worked if the manager was trusted but, if they weren't, it's unlikely that they would have high enough EI to make the necessary observations in the first place!

Though we hate to admit it, she realized, our bosses can change the emotional tone of our day with a couple of words, either encouraging or critical. Thus, it is extremely important for those in charge to watch how they reinforce their employees' behaviour and maintain consistency. Inconsistent bosses can turn a great employee who is excited to come to work every day into a disgruntled, nonplussed employee who allows himself, or herself, to become complacent and disinterested.

If a boss changes his tune on a daily basis, an employee will become confused. If an employee receives a "Great job!" one day and then a nitpicking criticism the next on a similar performance, the employee won't have a clear idea of how to succeed. Of course the boss may not have any idea that he did any damage. He may have spilled coffee on himself on the way to work, someone may have looked at him the wrong way, or maybe there is trouble at home. Then, he arrived at work, saw a small error in the employee's performance and – instead of leading with the positive – told the employee the small thing that was wrong. The boss returns to his work, clueless of the damage that was just inflicted; the employee returns to her desk, dejected and baffled.

Over time, repetitive inconsistent behaviour like this can lead to learned helplessness in the employee. Essentially learned helplessness means the employee once thought of herself as competent and good at what she does, but because of her boss's inconsistent reinforcement, her opinion of herself degenerates and she begins to think of herself as incompetent. This of course can all be avoided by self-awareness on the part of the boss.

But even those bosses who are self-aware and skilled enough to be of use to their colleagues have to believe it worthwhile taking the time out of their day to do so. They have to believe that helping people get better not only feels good but that it's part of their job (a big part) and will, ultimately, reduce their stress too.

"It is a lot of work," Debra acknowledged. "And it takes both skill and motivation but I'm determined to do what it takes so that, in the future, I'm prepared to help others like Johann has helped me."

 Key Takeaways

1. *It is extremely important for bosses to watch how they reinforce their employees' behaviour and maintain consistency.*

2. *Repetitive inconsistent behaviour on the part of the boss can lead to learned helplessness in the employee.*

3. *Learned helplessness in the employee can be avoided by self-awareness on the part of the boss.*

4. *Believe that helping people improve not only feels good, but that it's a big part of your job and will ultimately reduce stress too.*

15

Understanding the Importance of Culture and Strong Leadership in the Matrix

D ebra's next session with Johann was mostly about a situation she was facing where she thought EI might be helpful.

Towards the end, however, Debra brought Johann back to a point they had touched on earlier – the importance of the manager and their manager and their manager's manager.

"In other words the culture," Johann said. "Culture is simply 'the way we do things around here' or 'what behaviours get rewarded and what gets punished'. So of course the culture is important. An intelligent person with high EI can attend every training course going, be mentored and coached and use these tools diligently. But if she constantly comes up against a culture where behaviours are allowed, or even encouraged, to limit people from using their EI tools for the good of the company, then eventually she will stop using them to the detriment of her work and the company. Or she may turn to 'the dark side'." Johann dropped his voice and impersonated a movie trailer voice-over.

"And although we're all responsible for culture I think it's true that 'the fish rots from the head,' so the senior management have a real role to play. If the boss's response to the most mild-mannered question is to start shouting and spitting or to ignore it then don't be surprised if people learn not to use at least some of the tools that build EI.

"And it's self-fulfilling – once that culture is there it doesn't change. Newcomers adapt to it – they get contaminated until that's 'just how it is' and nobody even questions it any more. And it's hard to get people to challenge culture but 'that's just how it is'. Have you heard about the experiment with bananas and gorillas?"

Debra shook her head no.

"A group of seven gorillas were in a cage. The researchers would lower bananas into the cage and, when the gorillas made a move for the bananas, they started squirting the gorillas with cold water. Moreover, when any one of the group went for a banana they all got soaked. After a while, unsurprisingly you might think, they stopped going for the bananas.

"Then they swapped one gorilla out and put another one in. The bananas were lowered in and the new one went for it getting himself and the others soaked. Very soon it learnt not to go for bananas. They made a couple more swaps and, over time, the existing gorillas grabbed the new one before it could get to the banana and get them all soaked. Now the new gorilla didn't know why. He just got mugged every time the bananas appeared.

"Eventually there were none of the original gorillas in the cage and the researchers weren't using the water anymore. But still, whenever a new gorilla was introduced and the bananas were lowered, he would get mugged before he could move towards them. None of the gorillas, at this stage, knew why they did this, why they avoided the bananas. They just continued the tradition."

"It was their culture," Debra said.

"Precisely. It can be changed but the key skill in achieving change is to be able to talk about it and you need high EI and all the tools to do that effectively. I remember one guy I knew who joined from outside as a new head of department. The previous guy's style had been to keep information close, make decisions himself and shout when things went wrong. People had learned to stay quiet.

"Because he was new he could see what had happened and he decided the best thing to do was to arrange things so that people could feel comfortable asking him questions. He had an opportunity to put his very different philosophy across explicitly as well as through the changes he was going to make. He wanted to give people a chance to reflect and to see that he did as he promised. He also desperately needed them to speak up as, to be honest, he wasn't completely sure what he was doing on the technical side, and so he was relying on their expertise.

"The new guy got an external facilitator in to ask the questions anonymously and then interview him so that everyone felt comfortable. He had a chance to prepare and the format made it seem more intimate than the usual speech."

"But he's unusual?"

"Unfortunately, I think so. It seems obvious that people could be working better together and so save themselves grief and time. Everyone agrees with that statement, but it's really only the great ones who actually put their time and effort into the work of improving how they and their team and their organization communicate, collaborate and manage better. A client of Patrick Lencioni says something in his book *The Five Dysfunctions of a Team*: essentially 'people think it's beneath them' and I'm sure he's right.

"But the great thing is that EI works. And it works for good reasons. It works because if you use these tools you become trustworthy and known as a good listener who thinks about the impact she has on others. Someone who can acknowledge different circumstances and change when appropriate. That is always going to be a good thing! Not that EI is a magic bullet! It's just the best thing I've found so far."

"I always see culture described as 'how we behave when no-one is looking,' which links to your point about it being about behaviour. But it's about values too, right?" Debra asked.

"Yes, but values lead to emotions and emotions lead to behaviour. At least, real values do. Not the values that you see on so many company websites that are just words or, at best, aspirations. You said at some stage that one big issue in the matrix is people not knowing what to do because they are accountable to more than one person. Isn't that often the case? I mean, aren't we often forced to choose between different options? Between the customer, the boss, the spouse, the kids, the car or the holiday and so on. How do people know the right thing to do outside work? In my opinion it's about values and culture. How else could they know the right thing to do? If the culture is strong and leadership is clear on the values, then the behaviour is there and that is much more powerful than the 'do what I say not what I do' approach where everyone is talking about team work and accountability even though a blind man can see that those things aren't happening. And everyone knows it. Imagine the level of trust in that kind of organization!

"Managing culture getting people to behave differently, to use different tools is hard but you use the same EI tools:

1. Use your senses
2. Consider emotions
3. Reflect what you notice
4. Acknowledge what you hear
5. Incorporate what you learn
6. Reiterate what you heard – people like to feel heard and it gives you a chance to check your understanding
7. Check for confirmation
8. Change when there's a better idea
9. Know why you do things, ask others
10. Review regularly
11. Ask "so what?"
12. Look out for obstacles – acknowledge and abolish barriers where possible
13. Calibrate – forces consideration of perspective, helps with predicting over time
14. Focus on the other person and yourself

And, of course,

15. Do what you say you will

"And you keep talking about it, reflecting on how you're doing and trying to think of new ways of getting better."

"So you don't become the gorillas." Debra suggested smiling.

"And the bigger you get the more important the culture thing is. If I work in a global organization where I'm constantly on different project teams then I'm likely to spend a lot of time in the storming phase of building a team and very little in performing unless the culture supports us all working together.

"Some of the consulting firms do it well – they don't start from scratch every time a new project or engagement starts. Instead, they invest time upfront so that everyone 'speaks the same language' and understands exactly what behaviours are accepted. They don't throw a newbie out into the field until they are absorbed internally, until they really live the culture. These firms understand how disruptive it can be."

"And consultants are notoriously insecure people. Bright but insecure and so always trying to fit in. Maybe that's the key to high EI – wanting to fit in?" Debra laughed.

Johann let this comment slide. "So we can spend time on developing a culture that supports all the things we want and need when we're in a matrix. It supports us using the tools so that we can build an effective team across functions. Then we can train people so that they know what EI is and how it can help them. And we can give them some time to learn about the tools and to practise using them. After that it's up to the individual although if we're serious we can support her by helping to find great mentors. Maybe this can extend to helping peers and senior management to become great mentors as well.

"It's an iterative process and a messy one because the tools you use to improve your EI also need EI to be used effectively. This chicken and egg situation might help to explain why everybody isn't more focused on it." Johann's voice trailed off as he pondered, yet again, why something so obvious and so useful wasn't better used by business and especially by matrix organizations.

Debra looked at her watch and, realizing time was nearly up, started to get ready to leave. Johann started.

"It's a conundrum," he murmured before saying, in a louder voice, "OK. We need to practise using the tools – so during the week have a think about which you most want to focus on and why and we'll start doing so at our next session. Good luck! See you next week."

"You haven't given me the list yet," Debra protested.

"But I saw you taking notes." Johann moved towards the door again.

"Yes, but that doesn't have all the detail that you talked about – how it can be used, top tips."

"No. And I will give you that list. Just not yet. That would be too easy."

"OK. Fair enough. But I thought easier was better and so I've played around with the 14 tools to try and make them easier to remember. I've tried to keep the meaning the same but change the words so that they make an acronym that might be helpful in remembering them. Here." Debra showed the new list to Johann.

1.	**B**e aware of your emotions
2.	**U**se your senses
3.	**I**ncorporate what you learn
4.	**L**earn to reflect your observations
5.	**D**emonstrate that you've noticed
6.	**C**heck by reiterating what you hear
7.	**A**ffirm your conclusions
8.	**R**econsider your alternatives
9.	**E**ngage with purpose
10.	**E**nquire "So what?"
11.	**R**eview regularly
12.	**A**nticipate the obstacles
13.	**R**ecalibrate for different people
14.	**C**onsider others as well as yourself

"Ah, it spells out BUILD CAREER ARC," Johann exclaimed. "That's fantastic. Thank you very much! You're still not getting the full list though!"

Debra was still trying to persuade Johann as he closed the door and sat down again at his desk ready for his next mentoring session.

Key Takeaways

1. *Be prepared to put the time and effort into the work of improving how you and your team and your organization communicate, collaborate and manage better.*

2. *Spend time on developing a culture that supports all the things people want and need in a matrix, by using the 15 tools in order to build effective teams across different functions.*

3. *It's hard to challenge a culture, but the key to change this is to be able to talk about it.*

4. *If people come up against a culture that prevents them from using the EI tools, then they will likely stop using them altogether. Remember the gorilla experiment!*

5. *Think "BUILD CAREER ARC" as you continue to practise using the tools to survive and thrive in the matrix.*

Epilogue

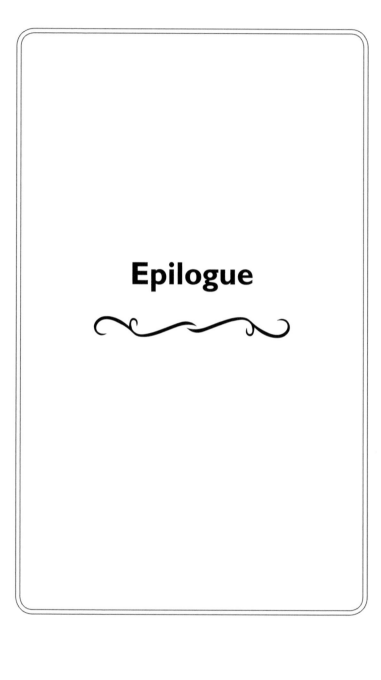

Everyone in a matrix, and some would say everyone who works in a modern economy, must be ready for high mobility, work with confused or multiple hierarchies and be able to assimilate multiple perspectives. They must collaborate, communicate and persuade; often across geography and function with all the attendant multicultural and language issues.

Having high practical EI, that is the ability and desire to use a range of tools to notice, manage and use emotions so that you can influence your behaviour and that of others is fundamental to success in these conditions.

High practical EI allows us to manage ourselves and others so that we can achieve our goals and help them achieve theirs. Pretending emotions suddenly stop at the front door of the office or after a certain grade is silly; ignoring the elephant in the room doesn't stop a rather distinctive odour from arising over time.

Using the 15 tools isn't difficult – the hard part is remembering to practise and doing it in such a way that you can use them at will and with skill so that you get better over time and move up the rungs of the ladder. Ideally this would mean training followed by some kind of "buddy" whether that's a professional executive coach, a direct manager, another colleague or a peer. The key is that the "buddy" must be skilled and motivated. Other resources might also help like joining a group on LinkedIn or following a blog devoted to this subject as this will help keep the tools and the need to use them top of mind.

We often hear it pointed out that not everyone who succeeds in the matrix is a good person and not all of them are emotionally intelligent. We agree.

Sometimes our leaders are not good people. But that has nothing to do with their EI. Being emotionally intelligent does not necessarily mean being a "good" person although someone with high practical EI, i.e. someone using these tools, especially the most difficult one "do as you say you will do" is likely to at least be trustworthy. Even if the only thing you can trust them to do is evil!

We can still get things done if we ignore emotions and the impact they have on our behaviour, but it will cause us more stress and waste time and energy, and therefore money.

So, six months after they started working together, how do Debra and Johann feel now?

Debra has realized that mentoring is not for the faint-hearted; although Johann is supportive and on her side he asks her tough questions and holds her to account for doing what she says she will. It's tough and sometimes she doesn't like what he has to say, but she knows that it's useful. She hasn't drunk the Kool-Aid and still thinks that technical skills matter more; but she also sees that to lead successfully she needs to be constantly working on her EI and that means using the tools, reflecting on the outcome and choosing one behaviour to change to constantly be improving, just like an athlete or a musician. She's also up for a promotion again and working with Johann to prepare for her interview. If she gets it, and the signs are she will, she's decided that she will ask for some mentor training and volunteer to be a mentor herself.

Johann, on the other hand, has started to feel like it might be time for Debra to find her next mentor. He's pleased Debra has learned something useful and is practising it. He has always found it satisfying to help others broaden their perspective and to understand the way they can impact their world. And he has always learned more than he's taught. He hopes Debra will find the same thing when, as he hopes, she decides to "pay it forward" and volunteer to mentor too. As for him? He was energized to meet the next person to walk through the door. And pleased that he didn't have to eat humble pie in front of the CFO.

Acknowledgements

The joy of my job is that part of it is to go away and research things that my clients don't have time to because of their jobs. A couple of years ago I noticed that the challenges of working in a matrix were coming up more and more often and the research I did next became this book. No book is written alone, of course, and the following people, in particular, were kind enough to not only give up their time and expertise to be formally interviewed to help me consider what it meant to work in the matrix and the solutions – they also agreed to be named:

Jamie Foust, Kroshina Rodrigues, Sean Murphy, Tony Kelly, Keith Carrol, Kashif Arbab, Florian Dubaoi, Paul Eid, Gavin Maxell, Rob Maddock, Priya Sarma, Samra Haboosh, Muhra Al Ali, Simon Baig, Roger Daynes, Hannah Bradley, Steven Greenfield, Abdirazak Suldan, Brett Preston, Yves Aubourg, Nick Fisher, Sean Kelly, Andrea Studlik, Assaf Al Qureshi, Samer Khalidi, Dave Tredinnick, Ingrid Flores, Dave Michalski.

And then there are the people who have helped me along the way either from near or far. They are far too many to mention but include Peter Burditt, Betty Sugarman, David Bradford, Juan Algar and Harry Hanscomb.

A number of people kindly offered to read the various drafts along the way and those who were unlucky enough to be taken up on the offer included Monica Amorose, Katharine Birbalsingh, Martin Braddock, Dorota Lewis, Mike Cunningham and Harry Hanscomb.

I'd also like to thank the whole team at Wiley who were very patient and gracious with special mention of Matt Santaspirt.

Writing a book takes time and my parents, in particular, didn't grumble about only getting a short time with me on their 40th wedding anniversary so thanks, Mum and Dad!

I was lucky enough to be able to write sitting looking at the beautiful lagoon in Sri Lanka and Elle and Dee deserve a special mention too as their wilful puppy behaviour provided plenty of fuel for the procrastination engine this book turned me into!

All of the mistakes are my own of course.

About the Author

Dawn Metcalfe is the Managing Director of Performance Development Services (PDS) and an experienced trainer, facilitator and coach who works across a wide range of industries.

Her clients are usually already highly effective and skilled people who wish to consider new tools that might help them as they face their next challenge.

Dawn has extensive experience of working with different cultures having lived and worked in the UK, France, Spain, Japan, China and now Dubai where she is based.

Dawn works regularly with board directors, senior managers and top management teams across the region to improve performance by changing the way individuals and groups see the world and the impact they have on it and others.

Performance Development Services (PDS) helps individuals, teams and organizations change behaviour and improve performance through 1:1 Executive Coaching or delivering Leadership and Management Development Programmes.

Useful Resources

The following authors of books, articles and blogs all have interesting and useful things to say about working in complex corporate environments and/or emotional intelligence:

Liz Ryan http://www.linkedin.com/in/lizryan
Lucy Kellaway http://en.wikipedia.org/wiki/Lucy_Kellaway
Patrick Lencioni https://www.tablegroup.com/pat/
Penny Trunk http://www.penelopetrunk.com

The books and articles referred to in the book are:

Crucial Conversations
http://www.vitalsmarts.com/crucialconversations/

"The Leadership Challenge"
http://www.leadershipchallenge.com/home.aspx

Emotional Intelligence (Salovey and Mayer)
http://www.unh.edu/emotional_intelligence/EI%20Assets/
Reprints...EI%20Proper/EI1990%20Emotional%20
Intelligence.pdf

The Mayer–Salovey–Caruso Emotional Intelligence Test
http://www.eiconsortium.org/measures/msceit.html

Primal Leadership: Learning to Lead with Emotional Intelligence (Goleman, Boyatzis and McKee)
http://www.amazon.com/Primal-Leadership-Learning
-Emotional-Intelligence/dp/1591391849